THE
HERMITAGE

PIERRE DESCARGUES

LONDON
THAMES AND HUDSON

TRANSLATED FROM THE FRENCH
BY KATHARINE DELAVENAY

CONTENTS

Author's Note

I should like to express my gratitude to the staff of the Hermitage Museum both for the welcome they gave me, and for the help I received from them in connection with my research. Many books have provided me with invaluable information. It is impossible for me to list them all here, but I gratefully acknowledge the debt I owe to the catalogues of the Museum edited by Somov and Benois, the recent studies of Charles Stirling and Germain Bazin, and the works by Georges Isarlo and Louis Réau, which were my primary sources.

Finally, I wish to draw attention to the important 'Catalogue of the Paintings of the Department of Western Art of the Hermitage Museum', published in 1958 by M. Levinson-Lessing, the Director of the Museum.

P. D.

THE HERMITAGE TODAY

Shortly after nine o'clock in the evening of October 25, 1917, Lenin, who, with the Bolsheviks, was in occupation of the Smolny Convent in Petrograd, gave the order to attack the Winter Palace. The cannons of the Peter Paul Fortress began to fire blank shots, followed by the guns of the assailants drawn up on the square and along the banks of the Neva, and finally by those of the cruiser Aurora, anchored in the river. The Winter Palace, seat of the Provisional Government, offered little resistance, except for that of the Junkers and of the women's battalion. By three o'clock in the morning all was over. The Government had fallen. The Red Guards were no longer the besiegers, the attackers: they had become Palace Guards. No doubt defenders were posted less to protect the Tsar's residence than to safeguard the priceless national treasures: pictures, drawings, etchings, and objets d'art, contained within the walls of buildings which were themselves of great architectural value. In a single night the Winter Palace and its annexe, the small two-storied pavilions called the 'Hermitages', lost all political significance; their renown was henceforward purely artistic. Orders determining the future of the country no longer issued from their precincts: but a living record of Russia's history, and with it artistic and intellectual treasures from the whole world, remained intact within its walls.

Petrograd is no longer a capital city; its palaces no longer house the Embassies of the world, and it is in Moscow that the fate of the USSR is now decided. Yet Leningrad has lost nothing of its lustre. The crowds on the banks of the Neva, the bus-loads of Russian and foreign tourists spilling out in front of the Palace, prove that in the USSR the present has not effaced the memory of the past. About a million and a half people visit the Museum every year. Foreigners are welcomed by interpreters, and groups of tourists are daily to be seen enthusiastically admiring and photographing on the ground floor, slackening pace a little by the time they reach the first storey, scurrying through the second-floor rooms in anxious search of seats and finally collapsing against the stone parapet near the exit where, flanked by the local anglers, they can rest their gaze on the sparkling surface of the water and the dancing boats.

Hordes of insatiable sightseers like these are, of course, the common lot of all the great museums of the world. What is striking about the Hermitage is the proportion of peasants, workers in their everyday clothes, and kerchiefed old women, who seem to have come as much for the sake of seeing the Museum as to visit for themselves the Palace of the Tsars. The pleasure written on their faces makes us realise how recent is the abolition of the Russian monarchy. The young people take it for granted that the Winter Palace and the treasures of the Hermitage should be at their disposal for the sum of three roubles, but the older generations are still amazed to find themselves able to walk freely about the Palace, even in the previously forbidden Throne Room.

The Russians visiting the Hermitage today are in quest of some kind of proof of the continuity, of the perpetuity of Russia in history and in art. In addition to the works of Western masters, the Hermitage has sections devoted to the arts of India, China, Ancient Egypt, Mesopotamia, Pre-Columbian America, Greece and Rome, as well as a department of prehistoric art, made up chiefly of archeological material brought to light by excavations in Soviet territory (for example, the Kostenki Venus found near Voronezh), not to mention a section devoted to Scythian art of the sixth century B.C., notably the *kurgans*–burial mounds preserved by the intense cold in the Altai valley of Siberia, in which a number of objects in bone, cloth and leather have been found intact in spite of the passage of so many centuries. People come to admire the collections of tapestry, precious textiles, weapons, ivories, pottery, porcelain and furniture as well. Painting represents only a fraction of the riches of the Hermitage; in fact the most popular section of the Museum is that entitled 'The heroic past of the Russian people', which is both a War Museum and a tribute to Peter the Great, the founder of Leningrad, whose effigy is everywhere in evidence. Even in the adjoining rooms, devoted to the war of 1812, are paintings of his victories, especially over the French, and his war trophies including the saddle abandoned by Charles XII of Sweden on the field of Poltava; there are also standards of victorious regiments, French imperial eagles, and even the coat of arms of Napoleon himself.

One of the rooms is devoted to portraits of 332 Russian generals painted within the space of ten years by the English artist Dawe and the Russians Poliakov and Golike. Here too is the great equestrian portrait of Alexander I, around whom the generals seem to form a guard of honour. In the Throne Room is a map of Russia (made of semi-precious stones, its cities and rivers marked in emeralds and rubies) which covers 27 square metres. This occupies the place formerly reserved for the monarch, the throne of Peter the Great being kept in a smaller, velvet-hung room.

While this part of the Museum is undoubtedly the most frequented, the neighbouring rooms devoted to the life and works of Pushkin are also popular. It is interesting to observe to what extent Art, Literature and History are combined. Peter the Great, Catherine II and Alexander are shown along with the works of Western artists and it is impossible to concentrate on one and take no notice of the others. Russian art is exhibited by itself in the Mikhailovsky Palace, opened in 1898. Such a division seems to reaffirm the isolationism characteristic of several centuries of Russian history. Until the reign of Peter the Great, no Russian prince could even leave Russian territory without an Imperial order. Foreigners were generally ostracised; vexatious regulations alternated with unexpected privileges. In Moscow, foreigners lived in a specially reserved quarter. The interest shown by Peter the Great and his successors in foreign art can be interpreted both as a reaction against this traditional policy and as a deliberate desire to copy the great royal collectors of Flemish, French, Dutch, Italian, German, Spanish and English art. Thus the Hermitage, as conceived by Catherine II, was able to stand comparison with the collections made by other monarchs or by the financiers of Berlin, Paris or Geneva, without giving any idea of

Russian artistic output, to which, since it did not rate highly in Paris or in Amsterdam, the imperial art collectors gave no thought. Until the year 1917 the Hermitage collection thus reflected not the aesthetic taste of the nation, but the interests of the imperial collectors. After the Revolution, it was augmented by the addition of the collections of certain former aristocrats and rich bourgeois, thus becoming a truly national museum. Its original non-Russian character was, however, preserved by restricting these additions to the work of foreign artists.

Although no regular programme of buying in the great auctions has been pursued since this date, the Hermitage collections have nevertheless subsequently been augmented by occasional gifts and legacies. But this has been a singularly small contribution in comparison to the fantastically rich harvest of eight thousand pictures acquired in the course of two centuries (two thousand of which are at present exhibited, while six thousand remain in readily accessible reserves). For the Hermitage collection was built up in only a little over one hundred and fifty years—a fact easily forgotten in face of all its Leonardos, Cranachs, Rembrandts, etc. We forget that Leningrad was founded at approximately the same date as New York, and that prior to 1703 the site of the city was no more than a marsh across which the sea-wind whipped up the waters of the Neva round a small Swedish fortress, half-lost amid the mist and ice.

PETER THE GREAT

On May 27, 1703 Peter the Great laid the first stone of what was to become St Petersburg. His mighty figure can be seen in effigy in the Hermitage. Six and a half feet tall, dressed in silk, he sits behind glass, the wax face just as Rastrelli modelled it, a formidable tyrant but also a remarkable leader, and the first revolutionary in Russian history. He built his city by lashes of the whip and government orders, forcing whole families to work on it and live there. St Petersburg was first and foremost a seaport, a window on the West, but also a Russian stronghold in the heart of a wasteland where the Swedes had formerly been masters. The first buildings erected were, therefore, the Peter Paul Fortress and the Admiralty, which served as a naval dockyard. For many years Peter I contented himself with a modest wooden dwelling and never even saw the Winter Palace, seemingly constructed to his measure, in which his memory is venerated today and where we may still see his carpentry tools, his books, and even the little bag in which he put the teeth which, as a keen amateur dentist, he enthusiastically extracted from the jaws of all those of his entourage who complained of toothache. Most of his life was, however, spent among the vast construction projects and he enjoyed peace and quiet only in the garden of the little Summer Palace where he would often go to rest from the perpetual din of work in progress. Peterhof, the great palace lying outside the city, as Versailles lies outside Paris, was completed only a year before his death. He died, however, in his own city, in a palace on the banks of the Neva, next to the present Hermitage, where Catherine II later built her theatre.

It is often said that Catherine II was the creator of the Hermitage collections and it is true that the catalogue of paintings shows little trace of pictures purchased before her reign. But while Peter was not so passionate a collector as the Empress, neither was he so indifferent to art as has been affirmed.

There are, of course, a number of anecdotes depicting him, as in Evelyn's house in England, shooting at pictures (surely on a day when he was drunk) or displaying complete indifference to the precious objects shown to him at Kensington, where he is said to have expressed interest only in an anemometer. In Paris, on the other hand, he paid two visits to the Mint and to the Gobelins Manufactory and expressed great satisfaction with the tapestries which Louis XV offered him on these occasions. When laying out his Summer Garden in St Petersburg he insisted on filling it with statues and sent an envoy to Rome, to buy antique works. Louis Réau has noted a certain Captain Yuri Kalogrivov, who bought 117 pictures for Peter the Great in Brussels and in Antwerp. He also notes that the Tsar arranged to buy 119 pictures from the English dealers Evan and Elsen. What were these purchases? What sort of painting did the Tsar admire? The names quoted are those of Rubens, Van Dyck, Rembrandt, Steen, Van Ostade, Wouwerman and Bruegel; that is to say, all the favourites of Catherine II. But he is also known to have tried to acquire Memling's magnificent 'Last Judgement' altarpiece from the Marienkirche of Danzig, and he was also greatly interested in the seascapes of Adam Silo (1674–1757), doubtless because during his journey to Holland he made the personal acquaintance of the artist who had introduced him to the science of naval construction. It is, moreover, to him that the Museum owes one of its Rembrandts, 'David's Farewell to Jonathan' (p. 137), purchased in 1716. His taste for what would today be called propagandist painting – portraits and compositions illustrating the great achievements of his imperial career – has already been noted. This may appear to us a very old-fashioned attitude but it is essential to try to visualise Peter in the context of eighteenth-century Russia in order to grasp the truly revolutionary nature of his taste, which was for a form of art completely outside the Russian tradition; that is to say, unconnected with religious painting. Tsar Alexis had already tried to encourage the taste for portraiture, but his efforts had not met with great success

14

and Russian painters continued to celebrate only the glory of the saints and the Passion of Christ, treating both in an entirely conventional manner, devoid of any trace of the personal feeling that makes a Bruegel, a Rembrandt or a Rubens so valuable.

Peter I doubtless had two reasons for being interested in realistic and secular art. In the first place he knew that it enhanced his reputation if painters recorded his triumph at Poltava, and that it was excellent for his prestige to be painted in all his majesty. He did not underestimate the propaganda value of a picture. On the other hand, he liked art to illustrate the things which aroused his enthusiasm, which no doubt explains his particular love of 'seascapes'. Even as a child he had been interested in what we now call 'scale models'. Later he worked as a carpenter in the naval dockyards of the Netherlands, so that he regarded the boats painted by the Dutch artists not only with the critical eye of the connoisseur but with the satisfaction of seeing art, formerly devoted exclusively to the glory of God, extol contemporary reality, understanding of which was so urgently needed in Russia. If painting could testify in favour of practical technique, then long live painting!

So that, even if he did not love art for its own sake, at least he loved it for the services it could render. For this reason his aim was not so much to collect paintings as to attract great artists to his own country. His Roman emissary was charged not only with acquiring classical sculpture but also with bringing back to Russia architects, sculptors, engravers and painters. Numerous Italian, German, Dutch and French architects came to work in St Petersburg, thus conferring on that soberly conceived city its delightful diversity of style. What was needed next was artists to train artists, engravers to teach engraving, and tapestry workers to start a tapestry workshop. The Tsar just failed to obtain Nattier and Oudry as 'Chief Court Painters'. He finally recruited Louis Caravaque of Marseilles who, according to Réau, painted 'very lifelike works' and who worked for almost forty years at the imperial court. Peter the Great certainly knew who the best people were; when it came to founding his Academy of Sciences, he consulted Leibnitz himself.

He was also able to start collections of Russian antiquities by issuing an order prescribing the careful preservation of all ancient objects found in the ground. This order was the result of a gift of gold objects found in Siberian tombs (mainly belt buckles representing animals in combat) presented to his wife, Catherine. Excellent results were obtained, the Governor of Siberia sending to St Petersburg during the first year about a hundred torques and plaques. Today this Siberian collection is one of the greatest treasures of the Hermitage. The Tsar's appreciation of this 'barbaric' art proves his perspicacity, for it is only recently that the artistic value of the objects belonging to the so-called Altai civilization of the Scythians in the sixth century B. C. has been properly recognized. For a long period they remained the exclusive preserve of archaeologists enquiring into primitive techniques. Latterly, their beauty, too, has received recognition. The Tsar's decision to safeguard objects found during excavations may have been due to the purely aesthetic pleasure experienced in contemplating, for instance, a precious stone, or to the desire to preserve an important part of the Russian heritage. The motive is of little importance in itself, but the decision illustrates once more the excellent policy initiated by Peter the Great in matters of art, a policy continued and developed by Catherine II.

The Tsar founded two museums in his capital: in 1709 a Naval Museum was opened to fulfil his wish that the Admiralty should possess a model of every ship built. The Kunstkamera, or Museum of Natural History, was founded later in the house of a Boyar, who had forfeited his life for plotting against His Imperial Majesty. This comprised the usual contemporary collection of curiosities – quantities of minerals, sea shells, stuffed animals and even monsters, for like many other monarchs Peter I was fascinated by freaks of nature and surrounded himself with dwarfs and giants, which he had preserved after death. The Kunstkamera also contained a public library and an observatory. 'I want people to look and learn,' he proclaimed,

Portrait of Peter the Great. His throne can be seen beneath his portrait ▷

instituting an infallible method of attracting the public by offering each visitor a snack and a glass of vodka. This tradition was maintained even when the Kunstkamera was transferred, in 1734, into the building occupied for many years by the Academy of Sciences and which still contains the Museums of Ethnography and of Anthropology. The artistic account of Peter's reign shows a favourable balance: he did much to prepare the ground and to open the way for his successors.

Disorder followed upon the death of Peter I. Four Emperors and Empresses succeeded one another in the space of sixteen years: Catherine I, Peter II, Anna I and Ivan IV. His own daughter, Elizabeth, then reigned for a period of twenty-one years, during which the Winter Palace was built and the Academy of Fine Arts came into being.

The Winter Palace, subsequently enlarged by the addition of the three Hermitages, was the work of the Italo-Parisian architect Rastrelli (1700–1771), son of the sculptor to whom we owe several busts of Peter I. The palace took eight years to build, reaching completion at the time of Elizabeth's death and the accession of Peter III, who reigned only six months before being overthrown by a palace revolution. He was succeeded by his German-born wife, Catherine, equally delighted to find herself Empress and to be rid of a much-hated husband.

Only the shell of the original building remains, for the great palace was gutted by fire in 1837. Its façades show great diversity of style, some highly ornate, others extremely sober, the northern, eastern and southern fronts providing a series of noble and pleasing harmonies in green and white. It was on the west side that the Hermitages were later added. The Winter Palace constitutes a great baroque world of its own: 1,050 rooms, 1,786 windows, 117 staircases. It is, in fact, even bigger than appears from the outside. The statues keeping watch, as it were, over the city and the great stone vases on the roof, far from adding a note of solemnity, seem on the contrary, in combination with the upright figures and smiling faces ornamenting the façades, almost to greet the visitor with a welcoming gesture. Though immense, the Palace looks a pleasant place in which to live, full of small, comfortable rooms despite its ostentation.

The Empress Catherine, at the age of thirty-three, was full of enthusiasm for life and for the exercise of power. She refused to encumber herself with ministers and appointed favourites to office: her conception of authority appeared to be identical with that of Peter. She seems, indeed, to have tried to emulate him in all respects, succeeding so well that we ask ourselves whether it was not perhaps the country, the throne and the immense task devolving upon its holder, that inspired in these two rulers the same alternating bouts of enthusiasm and of anger, the same thirst for great enterprises and the same obsession with minor detail. Catherine made no secret of the fact that Peter's writings were her Bible. Perhaps she thought they would reveal to a little German princess the secret of how to govern the great Russian Empire. Elizabeth might be thought to have provided a more natural example, but Catherine was loath to model herself upon a mother-in-law at whose hands she had suffered so much humiliation. Yet Elizabeth's work in the domain of the arts was by no means negligible: the Academy of Fine Arts was a useful creation and her choice of Rastrelli showed good taste. We should, however, consider Catherine as she wished to be considered: in direct comparison with Peter. On the pedestal of Falconet's statue she inscribed the words: 'Petro primo, Catherina secunda', and indeed Catherine, shining light of the newly-created dynasty of Holstein-Gottorp, was to prove the most faithful successor to the greatest Romanov.

Catherine painted her own portrait very justly in an epitaph that she wrote for herself during the Carnival of 1778: 'Here lies Catherine II. Born in Stettin on April 21, 1729. Came to Russia in 1744 to marry Peter III. At the age of fourteen she made a triple vow: to please her husband, Elizabeth and the Russian nation. She did everything to fulfil this vow. Eighteen years of solitude and boredom led her to read many books. On succeeding to the throne of Russia, her only aim was the well-being, happiness, liberty and wealth of her subjects. She bore no grudges and hated no one. Indulgent, easygoing, republican in spirit and kind in heart, she made friends, liked work, loved society and delighted in the arts.'

Nothing in our knowledge of her youth provides a reason for this passion for the arts. At Stettin she had been taught literature, deportment and music and her French governess had revealed to her, through the works of Corneille and of Molière, the charms of the French language, while her tutor taught her German. Nothing suggests that she was brought up to admire great works of art. Her father was not a very rich man. 'What do you expect,' she was to write later, 'I was brought up to marry some local princeling and I was taught everything necessary to that end. But neither Mlle Cardel (her governess) nor I ever expected anything like this.'

Nor was it from the Grand Duke her husband that she learned her love of art. She was sixteen years old; he was seventeen. The only possible explanation of her taste seems to lie in literature. At the time of her accession to the throne, the Chevalier d'Eon wrote these words: 'The Empress has a great love of reading and the greater part of her time since her marriage has been spent devouring those modern French and English authors who have written the most influential works on ethics, the natural sciences and religion. It is enough for a book to be condemned in France for her to give it her full approbation. She is never without the works of Voltaire the *"De l'Esprit"* of Helvetius, the writings of Encyclopaedists and of Jean-Jacques Rousseau. She is in fact a natural bluestocking.'

She herself was to assure Voltaire that: 'Since 1746, when I became mistress of my own time, I have been under the greatest obligation to you. Up till then I read only novels, but one day your works fell into my hands by chance; since then I have read them constantly and no longer wish to read any books except those that are as well written as yours.'

While certainly appreciative of style, there is no doubt that her main preoccupation was to be a liberal-minded and enlightened sovereign in a Russia which was rapidly evolving into a modern state. She wished to represent for Voltaire, Helvetius and Diderot the ideal type of Empress, and hoped that her adherence to European conceptions would encourage her people to adopt Western ideas and tastes. This is evident from her literary relationship with various writers and artists: from this correspondence she obtained all the satisfactions of a young provincial girl exchanging letters with the great men of her age.

She also looked to them to ensure her posthumous glory. There seems to be no doubt that she was fully aware of the importance to a sovereign of the praises of a great writer. Voltaire had written about Charles XII of Sweden. Why had he composed no work concerning his rival, Peter the Great? Perhaps he might write one concerning Catherine herself? Frederick II of Prussia had kept Voltaire at Sans Souci for three years. That was obviously the thing to do. Catherine immediately determined to enter the circle of these initiates, and no sooner had she become Empress than she asked d'Alembert to become her son's tutor and invited Diderot to come and finish the Encyclopaedia in St Petersburg. In the same spirit she collected Western art and neglected potential native talent, buying the works of Diderot and Voltaire and showing little interest in Russian authors, despite the creation of a Russian Academy. She admired the Parisian libertarian philosophers, but did not hesitate to imprison men of letters in St Petersburg. Perhaps the truth is that it is impossible to be both Slav and European, and that her real achievement was to have succeeded in Europeanising Russia as much as she did and to have procured so many masterpieces for its museums. History provides other instances of a passion for foreign talent combined with indifference to native genius; witness the ignorance of those American collectors so blinded by their admiration for anything that comes from Paris, that they remain completely ignorant of the work of New York artists. Such an attitude, unjust in our eyes, probably causes no qualms in the minds of those who adopt it. Our lives are full of similar contradictions and Catherine certainly found it just as normal, after reading a letter from Voltaire, to read in the St Petersburg Gazette announcements such as these: 'Sixteen-year-old peasant girl for sale, well behaved, price 20 roubles,' or 'Good musician for sale, excellent conductor, price 800 roubles,' as she did, a few days later, to buy the collection of the Count de Brühl in Dresden for 180,000 roubles. After the Seven Years War, during which she had refused to reverse the alliances planned by her husband before his death, she entered into negotiations with the dealer Gotkowski.

This gentleman also regularly supplied pictures to Frederick II of Prussia, who had done so much to further Catherine's marriage (which, incidentally, in no way inhibited her from calling him her mortal enemy once she was on the throne, nor yet from subsequently signing a Treaty of Alliance with him: she had, in fact, lost no time in mastering the rules of politics). Gotskowski was in debt and Catherine was delighted to strike a bargain with him and thus to secure for herself in Berlin itself 225 pictures which should normally have gone to Sans Souci to delight the eyes of Frederick. Spite may, indeed, have been the mainspring of Catherine's love of art collecting. Gotskowski's collection was mixed but comprised several Rembrandts (The 'Incredulity of St Thomas', 'Potiphar's Wife', 'Portrait of a Turk'), a 'Man with a glove' (p. 127) by Frans Hals, the 'Market at Amsterdam' by B. Van der Helst; two Goltzius: 'Adam and Eve' and 'The Baptism'; several portraits by Franz Pourbus the Elder, etc. It was limited to Dutch and Flemish painting, as was indeed usual at this time. According to the *Guide des Etrangers à Paris*, listing the collections of the principal Parisian collectors, published by the Abbé Thierry in 1787, M. de Calonne, for instance, possessed only eight Italian and eight French pictures to about fifty of the 'Flemish School'. In the galleries of the duc de Praslin, whose collection was said to be second only to those of the King and of Monseigneur le duc d'Orléans, the most valued section was also that of the 'Flemish School'. The same held good everywhere, even in Italy.

Throughout the eighteenth century in Europe the small Dutch or Flemish picture was triumphant. Van Luttervelt in his book on Dutch Museums provides an excellent explanation of this phenomenon: in the seventeenth century Italian pictures had become overvalued. By the eighteenth century none were left on the market: the great works of the great masters had already been collected. Connoisseurs therefore turned their attention to Dutch art. Rembrandt's works did not yet rival those of Raphael in price, and though Gerard Dou fetched relatively high sums, he nevertheless remained consider-

22

ably less expensive than Leonardo. Moreover, the realism of Dutch and Flemish art, entirely new to Russia, came at exactly the right moment to meet the aspirations of a society tired of finding in its own art nothing but repetitions of the religious scenes which filled its churches. The detailed still-life studies of the Dutch, the lively Flemish scenes, the noble sobriety of the Delft artists, might have been purposely intended to please those who were tired of the conventionality and ostentation of an all-pervasive religion. Moreover, the artists of the Netherlands generally confined themselves to small-scale pictures and this was greatly appreciated by collectors who could thus easily replace with the new loves the blanks left on their walls by the removal of the old. Art collecting was becoming as simple as book collecting and picture galleries were growing more and more like libraries.

Satisfied with her first purchase, and determined to organise her collection on a serious basis, Catherine ordered her Ambassadors throughout Europe to keep her informed of interesting sales and estates for disposal. Meanwhile, the fact that d'Alembert and Diderot had declined her invitations made her realise that however she might wish to play the role of the 'Semiramis of the North', her fame was not sufficient to bring the *Philosophes* flying to obey her slightest whim. She had not yet been admitted within the sacred circle. It was not enough to subscribe to Grimm's *Correspondance littéraire*, like all her contemporaries of good taste. Amid the endless building works of her capital, she was just one remote member of the reading public.

In 1765 her Ambassador in Paris, Dimitri Galitzin, a friend of the *Philosophes* and a habitué of the Salon of Madame Geoffrin, learned from the latter that Diderot was in need of cash and considering the sale of the library he had compiled for his work on the Encyclopaedia. Her Imperial Majesty immediately responded generously by making an offer higher than Diderot had asked and by appointing the writer librarian of his own books. Delighted to hear later that Diderot had included his own manuscripts in the sale, she paid him outright his salary for fifty years. Diderot thus found himself in possession of a fortune of 41,000 *livres,* and Catherine was in every sense celebrated in the world of the *Philosophes*. This, of course, made everybody happy.

The *Philosophes* turned out to be her best suppliers of pictures. By virtue of their position they were extremely well-informed about Parisian life, public sales, and the financial means of the various collectors. Moreover, they were often authorities on the subject: Diderot in particular, since the publication of his 'Salons' in the *Correspondence littéraire* (1759) had acquired a reputation as an arbiter of taste in the fine arts.

Thus Catherine's generosity was lavished on a man capable of rendering her great service. It would, however, be unfair to suppose that her magnificent gesture was inspired only by a fierce and obsessive collector's mania. Indeed, she did not look so far ahead; her immediate aim was simply to cut a figure in the intellectual world. Once admitted there, it was natural that her services should be solicited, that she should respond, and subsequently demand further services in return.

In the following year, 1766, Diderot had occasion to show his usefulness. Catherine had asked Galitzin to find her a sculptor to execute a statue of Peter the Great for St Petersburg. The price offered was 300,000 *livres*. Galitzin proposed the work in turn to Cousteau, to Louis-Claude Vassé and to Pajou. The first asked 450,000, the second 400,000 and the third 600,000 *livres*. Diderot then announced that Falconet offered to execute the memorial for 25,000 *livres* per annum and that he was prepared to devote eight years to its completion. This represented a considerable saving. In point of fact, Falconet's 'Peter the Great' took nearly twelve years to complete and was finally installed in 1782, in the absence of the sculptor, who, by this time, had quarrelled with the Tsarina. Ten years earlier Catherine had written in awed tones to Mme Geoffrin: 'He is a friend of Diderot!'

As long as he remained Ambassador in Paris, Galitzin was re-

Portrait of Catherine the Great, contemporary engraving ▷

CATHERINE ALEX.^{NA} II.
Impératrice et Autocratice
de toutes les Russies.

sponsible for purchases for the imperial collection. It is no doubt to him that the acquisition, in 1766, of a magnificent Rembrandt is due: 'The Return of the Prodigal Son' (p. 285). Little is known of the owner from whom this picture was purchased 'for Russia', but its story is highly revealing of the habits of eighteenth-century art collectors which, indeed, have changed remarkably little since. 'This picture', Somov tells us, 'was once part of the collection of Jan de Gise of Bonn. When his collection was sold in 1742, it was bought by the Elector and Archbishop of Cologne, Clement-Augustus, for the sum of 605 florins. When his pictures in turn were sold in Paris in 1764, this work was withdrawn, offers reaching only 3,263 *livres*. Shortly afterwards it was sold to M. d'Amezune in Paris for 5,400 *livres*.' From this we can see that collectors engaged in a veritable traffic in pictures, often keeping their acquisitions for the shortest of periods, only too happy to realize their profits at the earliest possible moment.

In 1767, at the sale of Jean de Julienne's collection, Galitzin purchased another Rembrandt: 'Portrait of an old woman with spectacles in her hand' (p. 284) for 3,401 *livres;* and a Gabriel Metsu: 'The Doctor's visit' (p. 287) for 6,020 *francs.* At the same time Catherine acquired a David Teniers the Younger: 'A wedding feast' (7,002 francs); a Van Ostade; a Berchem: 'Italian landscape' (8,012 francs); a Philips Wouwerman: 'Sea port (2,071 *livres*); Watteau's 'Mezzetin' (708 *livres* 1 *sou*) and 850 drawings by Callot. When Galitzin left Paris for The Hague, Diderot undertook to supply Catherine with pictures, with the aid of Khotinski, the new French *Chargé d'Affaires.*

When in 1768 Diderot heard news of the death of the ex-secretary of Louis XV, Gaignat ('who', he wrote, 'had collected some wonderful works of literature almost without knowing how to read, and some wonderful works of art without being able to see any more in them than a blind man'), he wrote at once to Falconet and to General Betski, Intendant of the Imperial Buildings, to inform them of the forthcoming sale. Catherine replied that she had already heard about Gaignat's death and its repercussions in the art world from Galitzin, but doubted whether she could acquire anything as the Duc de Choiseul was certain to take it all. Diderot insisted that he had been told by an excellent informant (Rémy, the Duke's agent) that Monseigneur had no such intention. This was not accurate and Monseigneur in fact bought up almost everything. When the sale was held in December 1768, Diderot was, however, able to obtain four pictures: three Gerard Dou and one Murillo, to which he added a Jean-Baptiste Vanloo, for a total cost of 17,535 *livres*. Soon the enthusiastic agent (who reported that these pictures were 'among the most beautiful in France') began to get worried. In April, not having received a single rouble, he complained to Falconet who acted as his intermediary with the Empress: 'It is a high price, but well below the value of the works. I am in the hands of the law governing the sale, and the law will not listen to reason.' In May, Catherine was able to reassure Falconet as to his friend's fate. The Bill of Exchange had just been paid and Diderot's worries were over.

This anecdote is worth telling, for it shows the relationship between the Empress and her French friends. A difficult relationship, because it was not conducted through 'official channels' and Russian officials were probably not always over-pleased with decisions over which they had no control. One of the difficulties experienced on the French side was to ensure that letters reached Catherine, whose post was scrutinized by many pairs of eyes, not all necessarily well-disposed towards such correspondence. Happily Falconet was there to serve as intermediary. For the Parisians, it was not a question of executing an order given by Her Majesty to one of her agents but of a friendly arrangement in the course of which each was free to offer his advice. Falconet thus passed judgment on Diderot's acquisitions. 'What a charming picture,' he wrote of the Jean Baptiste Vanloo ('Triumph of Galatea'). 'What magnificent brushwork! What beautiful tones! What a sweet little head of Aphrodite! What an admirable consistency! As for the Murillo, (a 'Rest on the Flight into Egypt') we should fall on our knees before it. Anyone who dares to think otherwise has neither faith nor morals. The three pictures by Gerard Dou (two 'Women bathing' and a 'Bather') are all jewels, notwithstanding the wretched, dry drawing and the colour of the flesh. After all, I do know something about it. It is practically my profession.' To which Catherine replied: 'I think you are right. It is only the Vanloo I cannot approve and I am well aware of the reason; it is because I don't understand enough to see in it all that you do.' This certainly indicates an unusual relationship between an imperial employer and a dependant artist. Behind the apparent mutual respect, there transpires too much warmth on both sides, too much timidity on the part of the Tsarina and too much amusement on that of the *Philosophes,* for us not to recognize the relationship for what it really was: that of a rich bourgeoise with bohemian artists.

The Empress had by this time already built her Hermitage, subsequently known as 'the Little Hermitage' to distinguish is from the Old Hermitage and the New Hermitage by which it was later to be flanked. Since it was, of course, useless to collect pictures without being able to exhibit them properly and since all the kings and nobles of Europe possessed their own galleries or *cabinets,* Catherine, who was in due course to have her own opera and ballet companies, her own orchestra and, for more private occasions, her own string quartet, had, of course, to have her own museum. Her plans were drawn up by the French architect Vallin de la Mothe (1729–1800) who had previously built for Elizabeth the Academy of Fine Arts and who, according to Sartoris, was spreading in Russia the style of Gabriel. The calm of his classical façades contrasted with Rastrelli's dancing baroque. What was an eighteenth-century museum like? Contemporary engravings show that in Catherine's museum one might have imagined oneself to be in the shop of the dealer Gersaint as painted by Watteau, or beside the King of France, in the midst of his collections. The walls were covered with pictures from top to bottom, in such quantity that it was necessary to invent a system of hinged panels making it possible to superimpose one picture on another and yet to see them easily. Such utilitarian buildings did not satisfy the architects, who much preferred, as Bazin has pointed out, to build galleries for decorations of a permanent type. It is only recently that the exhibition of pictures has been accepted as part of the architectural repertoire, and the building conceived expressly for the exhibition and rational classification of pictures has only just been invented: the pictures are easier to see, but fewer in number. The newer system is not necessarily the better. In a number of places, the Hermitage has preserved the original galleries. The high walls are covered with pictures to the ceiling. I have no complaints on this score and if those interested primarily in décor prefer the rooms where a few masterpieces only are exhibited in a setting reminiscent of the epoch during which they were painted, art lovers are inclined to regret that this elegant touch deprives them of many precious pictures. For this reason the Louvre has recently reverted to the old technique of closely-hung pictures in the rooms in which the pictures taken from its reserves are exhibited. The Hermitage, however, has never broken with the principles of Catherine's time.

One objection to the first system is that too many pictures are hung opposite the windows: if the picture is behind glass, as is often the case, it is difficult to see anything but the reflection of the Neva or the face of the person next to you. If, however, the picture is protected only by its varnish, one gets fewer such reflections and in any case it is always possible to find the correct angle of light. Such difficulties are only trivial; they may even, in the long run, be beneficial to the visitor, who needs a constant spur to his curiosity.

In 1769 Catherine brought off a major coup. She had just won a war against the Turks; now she won an equally great victory in Dresden by purchasing for 180,000 roubles the collection of the recently deceased Count de Brühl. This nobleman, minister of Foreign Affairs to Augustus II, King of Poland and Elector of Saxony, had managed to build up side by side with the royal collection (which later became the magnificent Dresden Gallery) one of the best private collections of his time of paintings, engravings and drawings.

Catherine has been accused of collecting only for the sake of display, of remaining as insensitive to painting as she was to music, to which, as she herself declared, she preferred the barking of her nine dogs. Certainly she did not, like to-day's collectors, examine her pictures with the eye of the specialist, interested above all in technique. She appreciated their narrative value, and thought that every picture should convey a message. Her fondness for describing pictures in writing was praised by Grimm, and it was in accordance with the spirit of the times; that is clear from reading Diderot. She has also been reproached for liking Rafael Mengs and Angelica Kaufmann. But this was a taste shared by the richest collectors of the day: the Prado, after all, possesses more than twenty Mengs.

There can be no doubt of Catherine's sincerity and of her genuine interest in painting. She herself admitted that she was less sensitive, even completely insensitive, to certain forms of painting and to certain painters. She did not, however, feel justified in setting herself up to judge the final value of a work. Her remark apropos of Vanloo should not be forgotten: 'I don't understand enough to be able to see in it all that you do,' she wrote to the enthusiastic Falconet. Nor should we forget the excited messages that she sent out on the arrival of a new lot of pictures. She had the crates opened and, viewing their contents alone in her Hermitage, told herself with the satisfaction of the jealous owner: 'Only the mice and I can admire all this.' Before long, nevertheless, she felt the urge to share her joy: 'My pictures are beautiful,' she wrote to Falconet, 'When would you like to come and see them?'

The Rembrandts, Rubens, Bellottos, Watteaus of the Brühl Collection were beautiful indeed, and well known to all contemporary collectors thanks to etchings of them. Their purchase by a collector as inexperienced as Catherine was a masterstroke: four Rembrandts, 'Portrait of a learned man', 'Portrait of an old man in red' (p. 284) and two portraits thought to represent Adrien van Rijn and his wife (now in the Pushkin Museum in Moscow); four Ruisdaels, two entitled 'River in a wood', a 'Mountain landscape', a 'Landscape with a dead tree'; 'The letter' by Ter Borch; five Adriaen van Ostades on the theme of the five senses; four pictures by Frans Mieris; twenty-one Wouwermans; two Teniers, 'The country doctor' and 'The amorous peasant'; and six great hunting pictures by Paul de Vos. The Brühl collection also brought five Rubens to the Hermitage: the portraits of the King and Queen of Spain, the 'Fight between the Centaurs and the Lapiths', 'Perseus and Andromeda' (p. 123) for which Brühl had paid 630 florins in 1738, and the 'Landscape with a rainbow' (p. 122) given to him by the Elector of Bavaria.

In the same collection were a few eighteenth-century Italian pictures: a 'Rape of Europa' by Francesco Albani; a great 'Building of Noah's Ark' by Guido Reni (p. 216), a sober work in which the two nude figures of a man and a woman are boldly drawn. The early eighteenth century contributed two big compositions by Giuseppe Maria Crespi. One, a 'Death of St Joseph', in which the faces are disappearing into shadow; only the head of the saint himself, already like a corpse, stands out, while a stick lying forgotten beside the bed bursts once more to life. Its pendant, 'The Holy Family', is at present in the Pushkin Museum in Moscow.

Catherine's Museum was now expanding. It is generally thought that she purchased only Old Masters, but the truth is, that, like many other collectors of her time, she saw no gap between old and modern art: people were as ready to collect Watteau as Rembrandt, and Brühl's collection included Bellotto as well as Rubens.

Catherine would have liked Bellotto to come to St Petersburg. She hoped that he would paint her city as he had painted Venice, and as Canaletto was then painting London. Bellotto had been Court Painter in Dresden, and in Vienna. He hesitated for some time but finally refused, as Oudry and Nattier before him had refused the invitation of Peter I. Stanislaus II of Poland triumphed over the Semiramis of the North, and Bellotto went to work in Warsaw, where he died in 1780.

Catherine was thus forced to make do with his pictures. The Brühl collection brought her a series of Dresden landscapes, depicting not only the architectural beauties of the city but also the life of the court and of the streets. Bellotto had a genius for portraying a city both like an architect working on a reconstruction and like a sensitive landscape artist expressing his emotions: his works are, in photographic terms, Impressionist landscapes 'brought into focus'.

The novelty of Bellotto's enormous landscapes did not put Catherine off: she had neither a predilection for the past nor prejudice against the present. Another advantage of the Brühl collection was that it increased the proportion of French pictures in the imperial museum. Watteau's 'Le Mezzetin' was joined by 'The embarrassing proposal' (p. 170) and 'The Rest on the Flight into Egypt' (p. 293). A Poussin 'Deposition' (p. 159) and a Valentin 'St Peter's Denial' also swelled the Tsarina's collection of aesthetic curiosities, while the drawings and etchings of the German minister laid the foundations of drawing and etching sections of her Museum.

In Paris, as we have seen, the departure of Galitzin had not slowed down the rate of Catherine's purchases of works of art. Diderot and Grimm had taken over, and the Salon of Mme Geoffrin where the *Philosophes* often gathered must sometimes have resembled a veritable dealers' den. We can imagine Mme Geoffrin, back from Warsaw, complaining of being unable to find a Vernet for the King of Poland, Grimm speaking of the Greuze he had just sent off to the Tsarina, and regaling his hostess with a new anecdote about the artist's difficult temperament, and Diderot waxing mysterious about the Crozat Collection, his hope being to avoid public auction and to send it to St Petersburg in its entirety. In the time of Louis XV there was no prejudice against such private business transactions by gentlemen. Brokerage, in fact, was perfectly customary in intellectual society. Rigaud had worked to enrich the collections of Augustus of Saxony, whose Italian intermediary was Count Algarotti himself. It was not considered at all in bad taste to play the antique-dealer.

Galitzin, appointed to the Netherlands, had kept in touch with the *Philosophes* in Paris, and willingly supervised the printing of their works at The Hague, continuing to follow the sales both for the Empress, and for his own collection. In Brussels, in 1768, he was thus able to purchase at the sale of the Austrian minister, Count Coblentz, forty-six pictures and six thousand drawings, among them many by Rubens. The six thousand drawings, added to those acquired from Brühl, gave Catherine one of the richest and most varied collections in Europe. Among the forty-six pictures were five Rubens: 'Filial love of a Roman woman'; 'Venus and Adonis'; 'Statue of Ceres'; 'Portrait of the Comte de Bucquoy' and 'The Virgin offering a Rosary to St Dominic'. The two pictures by Gerard Dou included 'La dévideuse', which had changed hands five times in the course of twenty-five years. At the sale of the Hasselaer collection in Amsterdam it had been purchased by the comte de Vence for 465 florins. When his pictures in turn were sold, in 1761, Jean de Julienne bought it for 2,567 *livres*. Six years later, at the auction of Julienne's collection, Coblentz wrested it from Catherine for the sum of 3,101 *livres*. His victory was short-lived: when his collection was sold after his death a year later, the Gerard Dou made the journey to the Hermitage after all.

The journey was not always easy. For if Catherine's trump cards were wealth and determination, she suffered constantly from not knowing what she was buying and from having to wait several months before her treasures could reach her palace. She could, of course, never attend the auctions for herself. She obtained only what her agents proposed, endeavouring to choose on the strength of the descriptions contained in the sale-catalogues. And once the picture was secured, it had to be sent to St Petersburg. The crated pictures were then at the mercy of seas, boats and storms. While the Rubens bought in 1770 at the Dufresne sale at Antwerp arrived safely, the vessel carrying the works purchased for 60,000 *écus* at the sale of the Gerrij Braankamp collection in Amsterdam the following year was wrecked. The only surviving picture was a Mignard, 'Jepthah's Return', which happened to have been sent by another boat.

Masterpieces sold after the Revolution:

Above, left: Titian, 'The Toilet of Venus', now in the National Gallery, Washington

Above, right: Watteau, 'Le Mezzetin', now in the Metropolitan Museum of Art, New York

Below, left: Rembrandt, 'A Polish Prince', now in the National Gallery Washington

Below, right: Rembrandt, 'Pallas Athene', now in the Gulbenkian Foundation Museum, Lisbon

The loss was serious, but Catherine was at that time living in expectation of the greatest prize of all: the Crozat collection. Her only comment was: 'Well there goes 60,000 *écus!*'

Pierre Crozat (1665–1740), known as 'Crozat the poor' to distinguish him from his brother who had acquired untold wealth from his Louisiana monopoly, was yet wealthy enough to have bought the sinecure of treasurer in France, to live comfortably on the proceeds and to amass a fabulous collection of pictures, sculptures, engraved stones, prints and drawings. Once a week his town house was the scene of a fashionable musical reception and it may well have been in his garden that Watteau, his favourite 'coming painter', conceived the idea of his 'Fêtes galantes'. When he died, his nephew, the Marquis du Chatel, inherited his collections. Surviving his uncle by only ten years, he left his treasures to be divided between the Marquis de Tigny and Baron Thiers. Mariette sold the nineteen thousand drawings and the duc d'Orléans bought the stones. The pictures had scarcely been divided up when Tigny died, in 1751. Thiers purchased from Tigny's heirs the pick of his share, and installed the Crozat collection in his house in the Place Vendôme. When he himself died in 1770 everyone thought the sale prices would reach record heights. Diderot, however, was firmly determined that Catherine should have the lot.

It was not a propitious moment, for Catherine was again at war. Her enthusiasm was, however, immediately aroused, and it was on the French side that difficulties arose. It was doubtful whether the authorities would allow these masterpieces to leave the country. In St Petersburg the cautious Falconet counselled patience. Catherine was in contact with Cochin, the engraver, and should on no account, so he advised, break off with him. 'His wide reputation as a distinguished artist, friend of M. de Marigny (Director of Buildings, i. e. of Fine Arts) and as a wit can make or mar the success of M. Diderot's negotiations. Once the pictures have been secured for Her Majesty, I can gradually let Paris know whatever is appropriate.'

In Paris, François Tronchin was already engaged on a detailed appraisal of the Crozat collection. While he was thus examining hundreds of pictures, part of his own collection arrived in St Petersburg. Who was this François Tronchin? As the result of some previous confusion, Grimm and Catherine called him 'The-Tronchin-who-isn't-a-doctor'. He was in fact a native of Geneva, cousin of the fashionable doctor, brother of a *fermier-général* and owner of 'Les Délices', which he sold to Voltaire. According to André Billy, he also wrote tragedies in verse which were refused by the Comédie Française. He was above all an art collector, that is to say that like all his contemporaries he dabbled in the picture trade to some extent and had sold part of his collection to the Empress. In August, Falconet, whose advice Catherine had solicited, had been to see these pictures for himself. He replied with perfect frankness that the 'Virgin' by Guido Reni was not a Guido Reni and that the two Bourguignon battle scenes were not among the better works of that artist. He also expressed reservations concerning the figures in two of the Claude Lorrain landscapes and reported that the 'Samuel in the Temple' 'painted in a fake-Rembrandt style' was a 'mediocre and rather nasty picture'. Only the two Lemoines (a 'Woman bathing' and a copy of 'Io' by Correggio) and a Van Dyck roused him to enthusiasm. 'Should I prove wrong,' he concluded, 'Your Majesty may be sure that it has been in all good faith.'

Catherine does not appear to have been annoyed that her Guido Reni should turn out not to be a Guido Reni, for she was well aware that such unpleasant surprises lay in wait for those obliged to buy blindfold. Her rivals on the Parisian and Dutch markets, Stanislaus-Augustus of Poland, Gustave III of Sweden and Frederick II of Prussia who, like herself, were absentee collectors, all experienced the same delights and the same disappointments. She was also aware that one person's opinion is never conclusive, and despite the fact that Falconet's remarks cast some doubt on Tronchin's competence, she did not attempt to get another expert for the inventory of the Crozat collection. Catherine knew when to trust people: when things were going well, she left them alone even if dissatisfied with certain details. As long as the successes outnumbered the errors she was satisfied: a policy typical of a potentate accustomed to active supervision who has learned from experience that it is impossible to achieve perfection in every domain. 'To deal properly with the fine arts,' she wrote to Falconet, 'one must have fewer interruptions than we have had here these last six weeks.' The 'interruptions' in question were at one point the Turkish war, at another the partition of Poland with Prussia and Austria. Catherine was, after all, a reigning sovereign.

Meanwhile, her Parisian friends had served her well: the Crozat affair was brought to a successful conclusion. On March 25, 1771, Bachaumont noted: 'The Empress of Russia has bought up the whole collection of M. le comte de Thiers, that distinguished art-lover. M. de Marigny has had to stand by and see these treasures go abroad, for want of the funds necessary to buy them on the King's behalf.' 'One picture only escaped us,' wrote Grimm. 'Van Dyck's portrait of Charles I of England, which had been requested by Madame du Barry' (who maintained that the du Barry family was descended from the Stuarts). Diderot, acting in the name of the Empress, had purchased all the rest, some four hundred pictures in all (Tronchin having eliminated a hundred and fifty-eight) on January 4, 1772, in the presence of the notary, M. le Pot of Auteuil, for the sum of 460,000 *livres*.

It was an excellent stroke of business when one considers that in that same year Catherine paid 30,000 *livres* to Mme Geoffrin for two Carl Vanloos which she had purchased for only 12,000 *livres*, and that, a few months later, the one hundred and fifty pictures of the collection of the duc de Choiseul were sold for 440,000 *livres*. Diderot was right in pointing out that Her Majesty had been able to acquire the Crozat collection for less than half its value.

The departure of the collection, despatched via the Seine and thus travelling to the Hermitage entirely by water, caused a great sensation in Paris and raised many protests. 'The collectors, the artists and the rich are all up in arms,' explained Diderot. 'I am taking absolutely no notice.' 'So much the worse for France,' he continued, 'if we must sell our pictures in time of peace, whereas Catherine can buy them in the middle of a war. Science, art, taste, and wisdom are travelling northward and barbarism and all it brings in its train, is coming south.'

It is easy to imagine the arrival of the Crozat collection in the docks where the Hermitage fronts the Neva. The voyage had been long, for the crates which had set out from the port of Paris in May, did not leave Rouen until July and reached St Petersburg only in November. And what were these long-awaited masterpieces? Among the most famous were Raphael's 'Virgin and Child with St Joseph' (p. 273); Giorgione's 'Judith' (p. 274) (then attributed to Raphael); four Veroneses, including the 'Pietà' (p. 275); the 'Birth of St John the Baptist' by Tintoretto (p. 275); 'Jupiter and Io' by Schiavone; the 'Portrait of an actor' by Domenico Fetti; the 'Portrait of a man' (p. 273) by Domenico Mancini; two pictures by Annibale Carracci, including his strange 'Self-portrait' (p. 276); a Cima de Conegliano (p. 91); Tibaldi's 'Holy Family' (p. 105), and Guercino's 'Vision of St Claire'. Catherine's Dutch and Flemish collections were augmented by a dozen Rubens, among which were his 'Bacchus', six sketches for the decoration of the Palais du Luxembourg, executed to the order of Maria de' Medici, two projects for ceilings at Whitehall designed for Charles I, and the magnificent portrait of the 'Maid of Honour to the Archduchess Isabella', seven Van Dycks, and eight Rembrandts, among them the 'Danaë' (p. 135); the 'Holy Family' (p. 139); the 'Portrait of an old man' (p. 284), and the 'Parable of the Labourers in the Vineyard' (p. 283), etc.

Thanks to this collection, the Hermitage also became rich in Watteaus (the Louvre possessed only one) by the acquisition of the 'Fatigues' and 'Relaxations of War' and the 'Characters from the Comedia dell'Arte' (p. 167). Catherine's collections of French paintings gained in importance by the addition of three Sebastien Bourdons, Chardin's 'Laundress', Claude Lorrain's 'Apollo and Marsyas', Lancret's 'Concert', the sketch for a tremendous picture by Largillière ('Meeting of the Magistrates') which adorned the Paris Hôtel de Ville until the Revolution; Louis le Nain's 'Visiting Grandmother' (p. 155); a 'Mass of Saint Basil' by the Toulouse painter Subleyras, and five Poussins, including the 'Triumph of Neptune' and Amphitrite, to which were added two masterpieces by this artist which Diderot had just acquired elsewhere. The marquis de Conflans, having again gambled away a fortune, was in need of funds. Who but the Russians would purchase his pictures? He proposed to Diderot the 'Landscape with Polyphemus' (p. 291) and the 'Landscape with Hercules and Cacus', accompanied by a 'Roman city' said to be in the style of Poussin and which was, in fact, the work of Jean Lemaire, the contemporary and friend of Poussin. Diderot did not hesitate.

Four months after the Crozat sale, came the Choiseul sale. Diderot spent 108,000 francs on pictures of the Flemish and Spanish schools. In face of these mass arrivals of masterpieces, Catherine decided that it was necessary to draw up a catalogue. It was to be in manuscript, for she had no thought of publication and visitors were rare, since she collected for her own pleasure.

Thus there followed another disembarkation on the banks of the Neva: the crates of the Choiseul collection, the spoils of a much dreaded rival at the sales, but not in fact a particularly rich prize. The 'Doctor' by Gerard Dou; Rubens' 'Portrait of Suzanne Fourment'; a 'Sick old man' by Jan Steen; two Teniers, and, to augment the Spanish side of the collection, 'Boy with a dog' (p. 151) by Murillo, the only Seville painter at that time acceptable.

The following year Diderot set out for St Petersburg to see for himself his masterpieces hanging in Catherine's palace, and above all, to see Catherine. From October 8, 1773 to March 5, 1774 he stayed in the palace of the Chamberlain Marishkin, since Falconet said he had no room to put him up. In the course of some sixty private conversations, the Empress and the *Philosophe* discussed everything of conceivable common interest to a writer and a sovereign, including the preparation of a Russian University and the possibility of starting the Encyclopaedia anew in St Petersburg. When the time came Catherine asked Diderot not to say good-bye 'because good-byes are so sad'. This was no ordinary relationship between patron and agent, client and supplier; if it could not be called a friendship, it came very close to it.

Once back in Paris, Diderot took a less prominent part in supplying the imperial collections, and before long it was Grimm who took his place. Catherine had met him at the marriage of her son, the Grand Duke Paul, in 1774. They were old acquaintances and she had long been a subscriber to his *Correspondance littéraire*. Above all, she felt more at ease with him than with Diderot. For her, Diderot, like Voltaire, was a 'great man'; Grimm was only a clever man. A correspondence of more than 1,500 letters proves that Catherine appreciated this, finding him much better suited than Diderot to the job of factotum. It was indeed to him that she confided the task of finding a decent lodging for 'Jacques le Fataliste' when, in his old age, he was to find himself sick and penniless.

After the year 1772, which had brought the Hermitage so rich a harvest, Catherine somewhat moderated her collecting ardour. In 1776, at the sales of Ganay, Randon, Bussy and the financier Blondel, she found nothing worthy of her collections. The Condé sales, however, provided her with one or two desirable pieces: 'A fortress' (p. 288) by Van der Heyden; a 'Music lesson' by Ter Borch; the Flemish reserves. But such minor acquisitions could not compare with the massive purchases of preceding years. This slackening in the rate of Catherine's purchases seems due less to a diminution of her interest in painting than to the fact that Paris no longer occupied the foremost place in the picture trade, an honour then in process of transfer first to Holland, then to Italy and finally to England.

Diderot had nothing of importance to propose to the Empress. She consistently refused his offers of works by Carmontelle, and Grimm had great difficulty in persuading her to purchase the collection of the comte de Baudouin. Perhaps too, her passion for Paris was proving as transitory as any other of her temporary enthusiasms. Above all, Catherine's other European agents, stung to the quick by Diderot's successes, had redoubled their zeal in the quest for treasure. Offers thus came not only from Paris but also from London, the Hague and Rome. This, of course, was exactly what she wanted, her secret ambition being undoubtedly to instal in Russia the master-pieces of all the greatest collections in Europe. She had already acquired the Brühl collection from Germany and that of Crozat from France. She was now ready to try her luck in the Netherlands.

Her organization was efficient. The moment a collector died, Catherine was informed. Thus when Govert van Slingelandt, one of the most influential Dutch collectors, died in 1778, she was informed that there was a possibility of overriding the clause in the will requiring a public auction. She might, in fact, be able to secure the whole collection. The French ambassador, however, was also interested, and in the end it was the Lieutenant-Governor William V, who carried the day with the heirs, by virtue both of his 50,000 florins and of the fact that his purchase did not involve the uprooting of the pictures from their native soil. Thus Catherine had to contend not only with exceedingly rich collectors but also with the growing feeling that works of art were the property of the nation, forming, indeed, part of the national heritage. The eighteenth century was a century of travel, and the travellers, as we have seen, were often also art collectors: every guide for foreigners now included a description of the galleries open to the public and their major treasures. Collections were becoming less and less private. More and more the educated man in the street came to regard the owner as a mere custodian. He disliked the idea of being deprived of 'his' Poussins or 'his' Rembrandts simply because the collector had happened to die or run short of cash. Catherine's purchases therefore encountered more and more national opposition.

All the same, a success in Rome compensated for the failure in Holland. In 1778, Catherine's Roman emissary, Reiffenstein, Director of the Russian Academy in that city, undertook to secure her a copy of Raphael's *Loggie*. It will be remembered that Raphael redesigned for Pope Leo X the decoration conceived by Bramante for the *Loggie* of the Vatican. Even the stucco-work and grotesques were designed by him and he and his pupils executed 52 frescoes – 'Raphael's Bible' – that Reiffenstein (whom Catherine dubbed 'Reiffenstein the divine' for his pains), arranged to have copied by a team of artists under the direction of Unterberger. The master-copier spent eight years at his task. In 1785 the copies (on canvas) were finished and sent to St Petersburg, and in 1788 the architect Quarenghi built the gallery destined to shelter this reconstruction. The Hermitage is thus in possession of a version of the *Loggie* extremely precious on account of its splendid state of preservation. Anyone today who wishes to make a thorough study of Raphael's mural-painting has to pay a visit to Leningrad.

Though Catherine was now buying fewer pictures in France, she kept up her purchases of books. Voltaire had just died and Catherine reproached Grimm with failing to have his remains dispatched to Russia, where she would have constructed a tomb worthy of his genius. Failing his body, she determined to have his books. This was not an easy matter. As Voltaire's great-nephew complained to his friend, the chevalier de Corberon: 'We have begged Madame Denis (Voltaire's heir) on bended knee to keep the most precious legacy we can hope to obtain from my uncle's estate.' In spite of her promise, Madame Denis sold. Seven thousand books bound in red morocco, almost all annotated in Voltaire's own hand, left for St Petersburg. At Catherine's urgent request, Grimm had checked that nothing was missing; above all, the letters which Her Majesty had written to Voltaire and which she was anxious to retrieve. Everything was complete. In return Madame Denis received on October 15, 1778, 135,398 *livres,* 4 *sous* and 6 *deniers,* as well as furs, a portrait of the Empress contained in a gold box decorated with diamonds and a letter from Catherine with the following inscription: 'To Madame Denis, niece of a great man who loved me.' Catherine had great plans for this library. Her ambition was to reconstitute Ferney in her park at Tsarskoye-Selo, and to house in it Voltaire's library and Houdon's statue. The new Ferney remained a mirage of the imperial mind, but Voltaire's books are still in Leningrad. For the study of Voltaire, as of Raphael, a visit to what was once the northernmost capital of Europe is essential.

The departure of Voltaire's library was far more than a family affair. Catherine's acquisition had been accompanied by a general outburst of protest. The French ambassador had come in person to register a discreet remonstrance. Since the scandal of the Crozat purchase, however, Catherine remained unmoved by such protests; she was accustomed to them. It therefore caused her no surprise to see her passion for painting cause a national crisis in England.

In 1778 she had, indeed, received good news from London. Her ambassador, Count Mussin-Pushkin informed her that the heirs of Sir Robert Walpole intended to sell his collection of pictures. Walpole (1676–1745), Whig Prime Minister for more than twenty years under two successive monarchs, George I and George II, and father of Horace Walpole, who, through his relationship with Mme du Deffand played so important a role in French literature, had throughout his life collected pictures in his family home – Houghton Castle in Norfolk – with a passion equal to that of a Crozat or a Brühl. He was also quite as rich.

It is almost as difficult to give an idea of the 198 works from his collection which went directly to the Hermitage as it is in the case of the Crozat pictures: a mere list of a few of the major works will, however, bring home to us the high quality of Catherine's latest prize.

From France: a Sebastien Bourdon; two Bourguignon battle scenes; four pictures by Gaspard Dughet who, at the Hermitage emerges as a great master elsewhere much underestimated, very close to the best of Claude Lorrain, but freer and therefore sometimes greater; two Claude Lorrains: 'Evening' (p. 292) and 'The gulf of Baiae', and two Poussins: 'Moses striking the Rock' (p. 291) and 'The Holy Family'.

From Italy: an Albani; a Bonifacio dei Pitati; two Luca Giordanos; a Luti; a Carracci; several primitives; a Guido Reni; four Salvator Rosas; a Solaino and a 'Portrait of Clement IX' by Carlo Maratta.

From the Netherlands: several Rubens: 'Jesus in the House of Simon the Pharisee' and a 'Bacchanalia'; a series of statues of the sovereigns of the House of Habsburg; six sketches for the street decorations painted in Antwerp in 1658 to celebrate the return of the Cardinal-Infante Ferdinand, and which, together with the sketches for the Luxembourg paintings and for the Whitehall ceilings, gave the Hermitage one of the richest collections of Rubens' decorative work; the famous 'Landscape with a broken-down cart' in which Rubens represented day and night simultaneously and which formed a pair with the 'Landscape with a rainbow' from the Brühl collection (p. 122), and a 'Portrait of Helène Fourment'.

As well as the Rubens, there were six huge Snyders: two 'Fishmongers'; a 'Fruit shop'; a 'Vegetable shop'; a 'Game merchant's shop', and an unusual 'Concert of birds' (p. 281); several Teniers and Rembrandts: 'Abraham's Sacrifice of Isaac' (p. 133), and 'Hannah teaching her son to read'; and a happy 'Family Group' by Jordaens. To crown it all came fifteen Van Dycks, including the famous 'Virgin with the Partridges', portraits of 'Charles I', 'Henrietta Maria', the 'Archbishop of Canterbury' and the architect 'Inigo Jones'. Perhaps the most important addition was the series of portraits of the Wharton family painted by Van Dyck: Lord Philip Wharton, Sir Thomas Wharton and their relatives. These bring to life a whole section of English society during the troubled times of the exile and restoration of the Stuarts, revealing something of the position occupied by the artist in English society; he was expected to be brilliant in execution and serious in intent. The pleasures of painting were to be concealed behind a mask of dignity.

England reacted violently to the news of the sale of the Walpole pictures. A question was asked in Parliament. It was felt that more than a collection of pictures was leaving the country: a chapter of British history was being crated and shipped away. It was recalled with sorrow that Walpole himself had refused to sell to the University of Oxford the 'Portrait of the Archbishop of Canterbury', which must surely have meant that his own intention had been to keep his collection for ever within the walls of his own house.

Catherine shrugged her shoulders and replied to Grimm as follows: 'The Walpole pictures are no longer to be had, for the simple reason that your humble servant has already got her claws on them, and will no more let them go than a cat would a mouse.'

These defiant words show that Catherine, like all collectors, enjoyed triumphing over difficulties. The more resistance she encountered, and the greater the danger of scandal, the more intense the pleasure she experienced. When, on the other hand, pictures were offered to her on her own doorstep she would frequently jib and turn difficult, complaining that they were overpriced.

The dealers who trooped to her palace doors therefore rarely met with much success. Many proceeded to show their wares to Falconet, to whose advice she seemed to listen. Yet even Falconet, who was entrusted with the imperial messages to Parisian publishers and engravers, often had difficulty in interesting her in works proposed for purchase. In 1773, for instance, when a dealer arrived with two hundred pictures, Falconet made a preliminary selection and suggested that she should buy 70 of them. 'Doubtless your dealer will ask a high price', wrote Catherine. 'Ask him how much he wants for what he has brought and send him to see me. If the price is exorbitant, there is every likelihood that he will take his pictures with him when he goes, however beautiful they may be. We have as good, if not better, and space is running short.' The dealer seems indeed to have asked too high a price. 'He is abominably expensive,' Catherine was complaining to Falconet a month later. 'He is asking 100 roubles for that miserable portrait of Monsieur de la Vallière.' 'If he is willing to take five or six thousand roubles for the pictures marked with a small cross on this list,' she offered a little later, 'I will see that he is paid.' The dealer told Falconet that his price was 8,000 roubles, adding that he was anxious to sell and left the details to the discretion of Her Majesty. Falconet in turn insisted that 8,000 roubles was not too high a price for 39 pictures, and the deal went through.

On another occasion Falconet's own son – an artist by profession – arrived unannounced in St Petersburg from London for the ostensible purpose of paying a filial visit to his father, but in hopes of getting a job at the Imperial Court. The Tsarina was at first polite: 'I have no objection to seeing your son's work. I have seen some of it engraved and it seemed excellent,' she wrote to his father. She was, however, mistrustful and suggested that Pierre-Etiènne Falconet should first prove his talent by executing the portrait of his father's pupil, Marie-Anne Collot. This he seems to have accomplished with success, for the younger Falconet was subsequently commissioned to paint three portraits: those of Catherine herself, of her son the Grand Duke Paul and his wife the Grand Duchess Natalia. But when the bill was presented, Catherine protested that, 'To put it bluntly, the price of the three portraits seems to me exorbitant.' Robinet's offer of seven pictures by Lemoine was met by a similar horrified protest: 'What, 40,000 roubles for seven pictures? Never in my life, thank God, have I paid so high a price.'

It took Grimm five years to get Catherine to buy the collection of the comte de Baudouin, an officer of the French guards. 'It is one of the best and most famous collections in Paris,' he wrote in 1779. 'Prince Orlov (one of her favourites) has seen it and I think Count Chenyshev is also acquainted with it.' Since this drew no reply, he returned to the attack in 1780, telling the Empress that 'The comte de Baudouin leaves it to your Majesty to decide conditions, timing and all other considerations.' To which Catherine replied in the following year that 'It would indeed be discourteous to refuse such a generous offer.' A year later she changed her mind again and told Grimm the price was prohibitive. Thus the deal languished until March 1784, during which time, in the course of a lengthy correspondence, the Empress alternately confessed herself tempted, and declared that she was penniless, in what appeared to be a genuine attempt to drive a bargain. 'The world is a strange place,' she wrote finally, 'and the number of happy people very small. I can see that Monsieur le comte de Baudouin is not going to be happy unless he sells his collection and it appears that I am the one destined to make him happy.' Whereupon, with no complaints as to price, she dispatched to Grimm the sum of 50,000 roubles.

Her first reaction to the sight of the pictures was favourable but brief: 'We are prodigiously delighted with the Baudouin collection,' she wrote to Grimm. Two days later, having presumably been told that her purchase had aroused much envy, she noted with obvious satisfaction that 'the great and important news of the purchase of the Baudouin pictures has made many collectors green with envy.' For Catherine, collecting was primarily a means of asserting power, of displaying what French tax inspectors term 'external signs of wealth'. She loved to dazzle and has frequently been blamed for this very trait, on the grounds that love of display is incompatible with love of art. Yet, her delight in exciting envy, far from differentiating her from the majority of art collectors, serves on the contrary, only to bring her nearer to them. The whole principle of public auctions, and the successes they achieve, rests to a considerable extent upon just such a zest for competition.

Certainly the Baudouin collection must have aroused envy: one hundred and nineteen pictures, mostly of the Dutch and Flemish schools, but including a fine 'Self-portrait' by Crespi (p. 277), in which the face of the artist emerges eager and watchful from the shadows; two pictures by Pietro Francesco Mola, a Venetian artist of the sixteenth century, and an admirable 'Morning at the port' (p. 163) by Claude Lorrain. The major item was, however, the nine Rembrandts. One of these, 'Jacob's Sons displaying Joseph's Blood-stained Coat', is no longer attributed by the editors of the Hermitage catalogue to Rembrandt, but to an artist of his school. Another, known successively as 'Pallas', 'Mars' and 'Alexander', representing a youthful figure in armour, a great helmet over the flowing locks, a lance in his hand, half-hidden behind a huge shield, is now in the Gulbenkian Foundation's Museum. Among the undisputed Rembrandts still in the Hermitage Museum is a picture showing a 'Girl trying on an ear-ring' (p. 285), her right hand cupped behind her ear, her left lightly touching the trembling jewel. It is an 'intimate' scene in which the artist seems to be allowing himself a temporary respite. The Baudouin collection also brought to the Hermitage a 'Portrait of Jeremias Decker' (1610–1666) (p. 285), with his frail body and rough face, topped by a large hat; a 'Portrait of an old man', 1664 (p. 284); and its companion the 'Portrait of an old woman'.

Ten Van Dycks have remained in the Hermitage, together with the 'Portrait of the Painter Jan (Velvet) Bruegel'; four Van Ostades: 'Village musicians' (p. 286), an 'Old woman', a 'Hurdy-gurdy man', the 'Lute-player', and a 'Fireside scene'. The Rubens included the oval-shaped 'Portrait of a young man' and the 'Portrait of Henry IV', also attributed to the great Antwerp artist. A Ruisdael, 'Road with a beggar', several works by Teniers, Wouwerman, Gerard Dou, Jordaens, Van der Heyden, Brouwer and Ferdinand Bol–119 pictures in all–brought the Hermitage inventory up to a total of 2,658 in 1785. Since the original 1774 inventory had numbered only 2,080, we can estimate Catherine's purchases during these years at some 50 pictures per annum.

Catherine was, however, not content with buying up, sometimes in face of great difficulty, the great European collections. Certainly these battles, these offers and counter-offers, gave her considerable pleasure, but she liked also to commission pictures directly from chosen artists and to follow the exhibitions in order to keep herself up to date. 'There is nothing in the Paris Salon which tempts me,' she wrote in 1769, 'not even any of the Greuzes.' Shortly afterwards she received a number of portraits by Vanloo, Vien, Casanova, and Machy, commissioned by Galitzin on her behalf. From Paris she also received the 'Attributes of the Arts' (p. 171), designed by Chardin to be placed above a door in the Winter Palace, and, from London, several 'Landscapes' by Thomas Jones and Marlow, forerunners of a commission given to Sir Joshua Reynolds. The choice of a subject having been left to the discretion of the artist, Reynolds chose 'The Infant Hercules strangling the Serpents', which was interpreted as symbolic of Russia's nascent power. In this work the great Rubens-like rhythms so pleasing to Reynolds are boldly manipulated in a brilliant play of light and shade, against which only the figure of the child stands out, the conquered serpent grasped in his fist. For this masterpiece Catherine paid 1500 *livres*.

Reiffenstein was entrusted with purchases in Italy, but his choice does not appear always to have been a happy one. 'It is incredible', wrote Catherine to Grimm, 'how the "divine" Reiffenstein has let himself be deceived this time. Please tell him clearly that he is to buy nothing more from Mr Jenkins: it is scandalous to pass off such miserable works as those of well-known artists. We are quite dismayed to see such daubs.'

On other occasions, however, Reiffenstein's finds delighted the Empress. Unable to obtain as many Mengs as she desired, he purchased a number of miniatures painted by his sister, Signora Maron. 'Order lots and lots,' wrote Catherine at once, 'at least as many as would go to make a basketful of little cakes.' But six months later she complained to Grimm, 'Why do you always want me to buy everybody's pictures?'

Were these alternating bouts of prodigality and economy in any way connected with temporary budgetary difficulties? Almost certainly not, for Catherine lived consistently beyond the national means. It has been calculated that revenue from taxes – including Peter's tax on beards – amounted to approximately 17 million roubles a year. Catherine's wars were ruinous. Waliszewski has estimated that the first Turkish war cost her 47 million roubles and the second 90 million. The upkeep of each of her favourites certainly cost her at least 500,000 roubles a year. All of which goes to prove that the price of Catherine's collections never weighed very heavily in so vast a budget.

Catherine's method of facing up to a budget of 84 million roubles, as in the last year of her reign, with such meagre revenues and such precarious loans, was simply to print notes. Her husband, during his brief reign, had found time to establish a bank and to launch the circulation of promissary notes. Catherine continued this procedure. It has been reckoned that she issued some 158 million paper roubles and raised nearly 300 million roubles by public loan. Any other country would have gone bankrupt, but it never occurred to the subjects of Her Imperial Majesty to lose confidence. However much the paper rouble was devalued, there was no thought of bankruptcy, which explains how the Hermitage collection came to be constituted without financial strain.

Catherine was not the only collector in St Petersburg. In Paris the Russian Boyar had replaced in popular song the image of the rich and eccentric English Milord, whose extravagances were sufficient excuse for their eccentricities. The splendid residences of Galitzin, Shuvalov, Bieloselski, Stroganov, Youssupov, Sheremetiev, Demidov and Bezborodko in Moscow and in Paris were decorated with precious items purchased out of their seemingly inexhaustable incomes.

They came to Paris to be painted by Greuze, Drouais, Oudry, Vanloo, Perronneau or Roslin. They besieged the auctions, ransacked the dealers' stores, and commissioned their funeral monuments from Pajou or Clodion. Madame Vigée-Lebrun has left a description of one of these glittering personalities. 'Bezborodko', she wrote 'is one of the richest men in Moscow and perhaps in all Russia. He could raise an army of 30,000 men from his own estates alone since, as you know, Russian peasants are attached directly to the land. When I visited him he showed me reception rooms stuffed with furniture from the workshops of the famous cabinet maker, Daguerre. The majority had been copied by his serfs and it was impossible to tell them from the originals.'

Sheremetiev ruled over 40 thousand serfs (or *souls*, as we know them in Gogol); he was a collector. Stroganov spent fifteen years in Paris; he too was a collector. Demidof was a collector, Youssupov was a collector almost to the point of turning his house into a museum. Thus the credit for today's Hermitage is due not only to Catherine but also, indirectly, to these aristocrats whose collections in whole or in part came to swell the treasures of the Hermitage after or even, in some cases, before the Revolution. Catherine's favourites must also be counted in the same category. To General Potemkin, the reigning favourite for fifteen years, we owe a 'Family portrait' by Corneille de Vos; 'Alexander and the family of Darius' by Mignard and two Reynolds, purchased for one hundred and five hundred *livres* respectively: 'Cupid untying the Girdle of Venus' (p. 290), a masterpiece of colour created by the artist on a theme which in the hands of any other painter might have been a mere piece of coquetry, and 'The Continence of Scipio'.

Catherine loved to inspire in those around her her own love of art. 'I am rendering a service to the Hermitage by undertaking to educate the taste of talented young men,' runs a revealing phrase apropos of her favourites. This excuse was not intended ironically;

Above: Da Vinci Room
Below: Eighteenth-century Italian Room ▷

48

she really believed it. 'He worked hard and improved himself. He had acquired all my tastes,' she wrote on the death of Lanskoi. 'He was a grateful, gentle and honest young man whose education I had undertaken.' By 'improving himself', Catherine meant not so much acquiring wealth as learning to appreciate beauty.

Following her example, her son the Grand Duke also took to collecting. 'The Grand Duke and the Grand Duchess', wrote Catherine, 'are stuffing their apartments full of all sorts of odds and ends of pictures and it gives me great pleasure to procure some for them. They actually have a hundred or so which would not disgrace the Hermitage.'

Even if Catherine cannot be said to have created a taste for art in St Petersburg, she did at least make it the fashion. It is doubtful if, without her example, the Boyars would ever have collected with such fervour. A certain feeling of rivalry certainly urged them to increase their purchases. The city now began to contain so many art collectors that several artists envisaged setting up their studios on the banks of the Neva and travelling dealers came to offer pictures and engravings, one of them even setting up shop in Catherine's capital. The house of Klusterman was thus able to sell the Empress a number of pictures by Berchem and Vanloo.

It was useless for Catherine to declare that she collected pictures only for her personal pleasure, that nobody but herself and the mice had access to her treasures, for the Hermitage had in fact already become a Museum. Besides which, the pleasures of possession, however genuine, are certainly increased by the admiring gaze of other eyes. It is only when one's treasures are admired and even envied by 'the rest' that pride of possession reaches its peak and that we appreciate to the full the privileges we enjoy.

By the end of Catherine's reign three galleries were fully laid out: the Little Hermitage, finished in 1768 by Vallin de la Mothe, the Raphael *Loggie*, designed by Quarenghi and opened in 1788, and what is now called the Old Hermitage, built by Felten between 1775 and 1784 by extending the façade of the Winter Palace along the river bank. In order to visit them, it was necessary to seek the permission of General Betski who, in the course of a long stay in Paris, had conceived a great passion for the fine arts and who served Catherine as Intendant of Buildings. The sculptors and architects who worked for the Empress (particularly Falconet) often complained to her on this score: Betski, they said, sabotaged their efforts. Catherine, however, never forgot that he had been instrumental in putting her on the throne and always remained completely faithful to him. Betski's decision was thus final. In the galleries, accompanied by the Curator, one might see not only foreign visitors, and Russian collectors but also students from the Academy of Fine Arts, who came with their masters to copy the pictures of their choice. This was one of the privileges granted by Catherine to students. They were, for example, also the only persons besides doctors allowed to enter female bathing establishments in order to find models.

The imperial collections were not open to everybody. But then that was not peculiar to Russia. In France, for instance, while royal and private collections were accessible to 'respectable' persons, it was only in 1750 that the first public exhibition of the King's pictures was organized in the Palais du Luxembourg. In 1765 Diderot suggested, in the Encyclopaedie, that the Louvre should be made into a Museum. But his plan did not materialize until August 10, 1793, when the Musée Central des Arts opened its doors. In Vienna, the Belvedere Museum was opened in 1781. In Holland, The Hague Museum was inaugurated in 1800 and the Rijksmuseum in 1808. Italy had outdistanced the other European countries by opening the Uffizi, in Florence, in 1737. The first signs of the democratic spirit did not deprive the sovereigns of their treasures, but it obliged them to share them with the public. But in her own time, Catherine, in reserving for herself and a few intimates the masterpieces of her galleries, was doing no more than conform to the practice of most collectors.

The Hermitage had two catalogues. The first, in French in 1774, was a straightforward list of pictures and was put at the disposal of visitors to the collections. The second, existing only in two manuscript copies was what is called today a 'catalogue raisonée'.

50

The pictures were listed in the order of their entry into the imperial collections. Each entry was accompanied by a caption, explaining its place in the work of the painter, whose career and personality were briefly noted. The catalogue order was not the order of the pictures in the galleries themselves, where concentration of numbers and over-all harmony seem to have been the main considerations. The position of the works was decided more from the point of view of the decorative effect than for their intrinsic worth; a system which, while in no way upsetting contemporary visitors, was in fact roughly equivalent to arranging a library in accordance with the format and colour of the books.

The catalogue was drawn up between 1773 and 1783, by Count Ernest Munich, president of the St Petersburg Chamber of Commerce. According to the present editors of the Hermitage Catalogue, this gentleman had a cultivated taste and a solid artistic culture. The attributions he decided on were generally correct. Count Munich seems to have done his job as well as, if not better than Lebrun, the first curator of the French royal collection. The Hermitage had come a long way from the curious labels attached to the antique statues purchased by Peter the Great for his Summer Garden: 'An old man with a long beard was entitled Sappho,' wrote Casanova, 'an old woman was labelled Avicenna and a young and amorous couple bore the names of Philemon and Baucis.' A few years only had sufficed for the Russians to acquire a surer judgment, and dealers could no longer count on the Boyars to buy those 'leavings' of which they were unable to dispose elsewhere.

Catherine's death in 1796 raised the problem of the administration of her collections. The Academicians were summoned and under the direction of Labensky, the new Curator of Paintings, they proceeded to draw up a new and more precise catalogue, including indications as to the location of each picture in the Gallery. It was estimated that the imperial collections, including those in other residences as well as in St Petersburg, then totalled three thousand nine hundred and twenty-six pictures. After only twenty years the collection of the Russian Court could rival those of other sovereigns.

AFTER CATHERINE THE GREAT

When Catherine died, her son Paul was so overjoyed to accede to power at last that he decorated the messenger who brought the news. His reign began amid a bevy of eccentric orders: even in his absence everyone passing by the Winter Palace was obliged to salute the Tsar's residence; any traveller meeting the royal retinue was obliged to get down from his carriage and salute it; all men were to wear powder; no one was allowed to wear round hats! Listen to the description of this mighty law-giver recorded by Madame Vigée-Lebrun: 'With his snub-nose, big mouth and long teeth, his head resembled a skull and his face undoubtedly lent itself to caricature.' She adds that in the domain of the fine arts he continued his mother's policy.

His actions did nothing to belie a caricature then making the rounds of the city in which he was shown 'holding a paper in either hand. On one was written "order". On the other "counter order". While on his forehead appeared the word "disorder".' As far as the administration of his museums was concerned Paul certainly bore out the truth of this parody. No sooner had he appointed a Director-General, Boutourline, and a series of curators in charge of the various sections – engraved stones, sculpture, etc. – than he set about dismantling the collections.

His favourite works were transferred either to his palace in Pavlovsk (built for him when Grand-Duke by the architects Cameron, Quarenghi, Brenna, Rossi and Voronikhin), to Gatchina, transformed by Brenna into a medieval castle, or to the new Mikhailovsky Palace, constructed within St Petersburg itself, once more in medieval style.

We are well informed as to Paul's taste in painting. The European tour undertaken in 1781 under the name of the comte du Nord, in the company of his wife and mistress, seems to have brought him to Vienna in time to witness the opening of the Belvedere Museum (this did not, however, inspire him to transform the Hermitage into a public museum). In Rome, St Peter's made an unforgettable impression on him, which resulted in the Church of Our Lady of Kazan in St Petersburg being built. In Paris he visited the studios of Houdon and Hubert Robert, of Greuze and of Joseph Vernet, purchasing pictures with which to decorate his palaces. He was enthusiastic over the architect Ledoux, from whom he ordered a number of plans. He also showed a certain liking for the works of Madame Vigée-Lebrun, perhaps in reaction against the judgment of his mother, who had signally failed to appreciate this artist.

Paul was subsequently strangled in his Mikhailovsky Palace; his reign was too short to give him a chance to play an important role in the history of the Hermitage. The pictures of Stanislaus-Augustus of Poland, who had sought refuge in St Petersburg after the partition of his country between Russia, Austria and Prussia, were, however, annexed to the Imperial collection at this time, thus explaining the fact that Fragonard's 'Stolen kiss' (p. 177) comes to be in the possession of the Hermitage.

Of his new, or newly restored, residences one (Mikhailovsky) was handed over to the civil service, another (Pavlovsk) burned down and, as we are told by Louis Réau, several pictures by Greuze burnt with it. Gatchina alone remained to provide problems for future historians of the Hermitage. Works of art accumulated in the palace without any attempt to record their origin, so that the label 'formerly in Gatchina' is often synonymous with 'origin unknown'. This is as true of mediocre 'genre' scenes by long-forgotten painters as of famous masterpieces. Once again the caricature proved true: Paul had introduced both order and disorder.

Alexander I reigned from 1801 to 1825. Labensky remained in charge of the Hermitage paintings and, in so far as relations with Napoleon permitted, Russian students were once more sent to study at the *Ecole des Beaux Arts* in Paris. The Tsar followed in the newssheets the changes of the arts in Paris. His own culture was French: the Swiss-born, Paris-educated Frédéric César de Laharpe, his father's general French factotum, had been for him a perspicacious tutor, with whom he had never lost contact; with the result that after the fall of Paris, Laharpe in his little castle of Pléssis-Piquet just outside Paris (now Pléssis-Robinson), was able to exercise a moderating influence upon his former pupil.

Catherine and Paul had witnessed a slow evolution in artistic taste. Alexander, on the other hand, lived in a time of rapid change. The familiar and at the same time intangible charm of the late eighteenth century was followed by a return to classical sobriety and gravity. The work of architects and cabinet-makers and of painters such as David was establishing the rules of a style, a discipline, in complete reaction to the fantasy and delicate virtuosity of what was already known as the '*Ancien Régime*', under which artistic freedom had been preferred to a rigid style.

Alexander I is said to have shown an interest in David, though not to the point of forgetting his role as a regicide. The Hermitage thus possesses only one David, acquired with the Youssupov collection. Nor was it, in all probability, political reasons alone which inspired his rejection of David, whose severity doubtless appealed to him less than the warmer style of Gérard from whom he commissioned his own portrait. Moreover, he ignored classicism for the romantic landscapes of Hubert Robert, of whom Catherine had declared, with bitter contempt that, since he was so fond of ruins, he should be glad to be living in the time of the Revolution, which provided him with fresh examples every day.

His appreciation of the architecture of Percier and Fontaine is evident from the façades of those Leningrad buildings which combine the elegance of the eighteenth century with the severe nobility of the Empire. After the Treaty of Tilsit, by which peace was re-established for a time between France and Russia, Labensky, the Curator of the Hermitage, went to Paris. There he purchased a 'Moses' by Philippe de Champaigne from the Choiseul-Praslin collection and, more important still, established with Vivant Denan, Director of the Louvre Museum, relations which led to the latter's becoming Grimm's successor at the Hermitage, and the new and assiduous purveyor of pictures for the imperial collections.

54

At the Giustiniani sale in Rome, the envoys of the Berlin Museum bought up seventy-three pictures, whereas Labensky, more concerned with quality than with quantity, acquired, among others, the celebrated 'Lute player' (p. 107) by Caravaggio, and the 'Crucifixion of the Apostle Peter', in which Spada reveals himself to be a very great artist. The treatment of this work in a chiaroscuro worthy of Caravaggio, the rigour of the composition and the realism of the figure of the Apostle, attain a truly masterly intensity and greatness.

As had been agreed, Vivant Denan took over the search for masterpieces from Labensky. He had previously been an *attaché* at the French Embassy in St Petersburg, as well as diplomat in Stockholm and in Naples and Curator of the royal collection of medals. He was typical of those fortunate men whose fine qualities and quick minds no régime can afford to be without. During the Revolution he was concerned with army uniforms. In his Egyptian campaign he followed Bonaparte, notebook in hand, bringing back with him one of the first serious works on Egyptian archaeology. Under the Empire he organized Napoleon's military parades and looked after the Louvre Museum, incorporating into its collections the many works seized from conquered nations. No doubt it is to him the Hermitage owes the discovery in 1810, in the shop of the merchant Lafontaine, of the 'Woman with her servant' (p. 143) by Pieter de Hooch. In 1811 he was still dispatching crates of pictures to St Petersburg. Between Tilsit (1807) and the declaration of war (1812), he enriched the Museum of Napoleon's past and future enemy with two great compositions by Murillo: 'Jacob's Ladder', in which the angels are seen descending towards the figure of the patriarch and 'Isaac blessing Jacob', a curious work in which we observe a skilful harmonisation of interior and landscape surprising to those who consider Murillo limited to scenes of sugary sweetness; a 'Madonna' by Rosso Fiorentino, the favourite artist of Francis I; a triptych by Maerten van Heemskerck on the theme of 'Calvary' (p. 282); a 'Portrait of Fontenelle' (p. 292) by Rigaud, and a 'Shipwreck' by J. F. Hue. When war began again in 1812, the pace of events proved too swift for Denan, and when Alexander re-entered Paris in 1815, the old man preferred to abandon the Louvre and to retire to his apartment on the Quai Voltaire, where he divided his time between his private collections and his friends.

In 1815, as in 1812, Alexander, hailed as a liberator by the Parisian nobility, sat to Gérard and visited his portraitist, Madame Vigée-Lebrun, member of the Academy of St Petersburg. This time, however, he could no longer go to Malmaison to chat with Josephine. The ex-Empress was dead and her collection was for sale. From Malmaison the Hermitage acquired pictures which the Tsar purchased for friendship's sake as much as for the love of art: among them four of Claude Lorrain's finest landscapes. These companion pictures: 'Morning', 'Noon', 'Evening' and 'Night' (p. 292), had previously belonged to the Landgrave of Hesse-Cassel who had hoped to save them from Napoleon's army by removing them from his galleries. Napoleon's envoys, however, proved too cunning, and the precious loot – the four Claudes – were presented to the Empress Josephine in 1806. The Cassel collection also involuntarily provided two landscapes by Jan van der Heyden (Cologne and Amsterdam); a 'Church interior' by Neefs and three Paulus Potters: the famous 'Farm' (p. 287), a panel grouping fourteen 'Hunting scenes' and a 'Wolf-hound' (p. 287). Cassel had also contributed to Josephine's collection a famous Rembrandt: a fine version of the 'Descent from the Cross' in the Munich Pinakothek, and three Teniers.

Alexander, to whom it never occurred that Cassel might reclaim his possessions, bought up everything stolen from Germany. He also took from Malmaison works of less dubious origin: Ter Borch's 'Glass of lemonade' (p. 287); an Adriaen Van der Werff; a 'Herring Vendor' by Gerard Dou; a 'Breakfast' by Metsu (p. 287) and a great 'Descent from the Cross' (p. 280) painted by Rubens for a Capuchin church. This work had been hidden on the arrival of the French revolutionary troops, and appears not to have been stolen, but presented to Josephine by the city of Bruges. Thus, in this particular

Portrait of Alexander I by Gerhard Lüchelchen, engraving by A. Tardieu ▷

ALEXANDRE I.er

Empereur de toutes les Russies

case, the Tsar's honour was intact—always supposing that collectors considered their honour in any way involved by accepting works which had been looted from conquered countries.

Alexander also took away a magnificent Andrea del Sarto: the 'Virgin and Child with St Catherine, St Elizabeth and St John the Baptist' (p. 273), a work of such delicacy that the brushwork has something of the facility generally found only in sketches, and a 'St Catherine' by Luini, which is very close to Leonardo. For these 118 pictures the Tsar paid well under the current price, although Potter's famous 'Farm' alone cost him four hundred and ninety thousand francs. So the spoils of the Empire found their way to Leningrad.

It seems almost as though the masterpieces given by Napoleon to the Beauharnais family at the height of his glory were predestined to hang one day in the palace of the Tsars. In 1829, the year in which her son, the future Napoleon III, attained his majority, Hortense, Duchess of St Leu, put her collection up for sale. Like that of her mother, Josephine, this was poor in Italian works (a notable exception being the 'Virgin and Child with Saint Peter and Saint John the Baptist' by Vincenzo Catena, p. 273) and in French pictures, despite a fine Fragonard, 'The farmer's children' (p. 294). The rare Spanish works included a tragic 'St Sebastian' by Ribera, an admirable study of two grieving figures bent over the arrow-pierced body of the martyr, high-lighted against the dramatic shadow in which the rest of the picture is plunged. The strength of the St Leu collection lay in its pictures from the Netherlands (Hortense had been Queen of Holland), and among works now in the Hermitage should be noted a 'Portrait of four children', in which Rembrandt's influence is perceptible behind the amiable hand of Van der Eeckhout, and a 'Family portrait' by Abraham Van der Tempel, formerly attributed to Van der Helst.

In 1815 Alexander purchased fifteen works of the Spanish school from the Dutch banker Coesvelt, one of the few collectors who had discovered a Spain different from that of Murillo or of Mengs. These two artists continued to enjoy the favour of the Spanish Court, but an austere and noble art, bearing no relation whatsoever to their facile and fashionable charm, was gaining in the esteem of connoisseurs. Among this collection figured also the second Velasquez to come to the Hermitage (the first, 'The drinkers', had been acquired in 1797), namely the 'Portrait of Count Olivarès' (p. 289), in which the artist shows the fleshy face and heavy features of his patron without any trace of flattery. It also included a 'Portrait of a man' by Claudio Coello, a 'Christ the King' by Juan-Bautista Maino; a 'Madonna' by Morales, three Murillos, a 'Miracle of the Loaves' by Pedro Orente, the 'Portrait of Don Diego de Valmayor' by Juan Pantoja de la Cruz; a 'Portrait of a monk' by Juan Pareja; a 'Portrait of Lope de Vega' and a 'Crucifixion' (p. 289) by Ribalta; the famous 'Virgin Mary as a Child' by Zurbaran (p. 147), and the 'Knife grinder' by Antonio Puga, considered by Georges Isarlo to be this artist's masterpiece. This last is a work of great severity and precision, entirely without artifice, bearing out the theory of the basic realism of seventeenth-century painting, on which point a comparison between Puga and Le Nain would certainly be of interest.

Alexander acquired other treasures for the Hermitage. Through his court doctor, Craighton, he purchased in 1817 a number of works by Dujardin and Langelbach and a 'Virgin and Child' attributed in turn to Giorgione and to Cariani (p. 97). From Italy and Paris, in 1819, General Trubetskoi brought back a 'Mary Magdalene' by Carlo Dolci, a 'Christ appearing to the Holy Women' by Annibale Carracci, and Maratta's 'Adoration of the Shepherds'.

From 1802 onwards, pictures by Russian artists began regularly to enter the imperial collections, which thus came to contain works by Lossenko, Matveev, Orlovsky, Egorov and Kiprensky.

It was Nicholas I (1825–1855) who transformed the Tsar's private collections into a public museum. Significantly enough, in the very first year of his reign, he inaugurated the National War Museum, of which we have already spoken. With every passing year the Imperial Palace thus became a little less the residence of the imperial family, and a little more a national monument.

Catherine II is undoubtedly the most attractive personality in the history of the Hermitage collections. Her correspondence enables us to see exactly how she herself built up this prodigious assemblage of great works. None of her successors entered into such close relationship with the writers and artists of their day, at least until the accession of Nicholas, whose artistic policy proved to be almost as generous as that of Catherine herself. He does not, however, seem to have manifested any marked taste for the great painters of this time, the only Ingres in the Hermitage coming from the Narishkin collection, while Corot, Delacroix and Courbet are also represented only by pictures acquired from various private galleries. Nicholas I admired the compositions of Horace Vernet, who was twice received at the Imperial Court. He also admired paintings of battle-scenes. He shared the general appreciation of contemporary German painters, sat in person for the English artist Christine Robertson, for the German Franz Kruger, and bought pictures by Caspar David Friedrich.

French art no longer played a preponderant role in Russia: Germany was now the arbiter of artistic fashion. The statue of the German archaeologist Winckelmann was put up in front of the Hermitage, and the frescoes by Hiltersperger which ornament the 'Gallery of Classical Art'—cold, stiff, classical scenes—may be interpreted as a naïve homage to classicism, to archaeology and to the learned author of *Thoughts on the Imitation of Greek Works in Painting and Sculpture*, from whom, no doubt, they would have raised a smile.

Nicholas I had observed that the imperial collections were overweighted with Dutch and Flemish paintings and conveyed little idea of the variety of the Italian and Spanish schools. In 1828 the arrival of the St Leu collection served only to increase this disproportion. In 1831, Manuel de Godoy, Minister of Charles IV of Spain, commonly called 'the Prince of Peace', undertook to sell a part of his collections, among which were several Goyas. But the work of this artist, underestimated by his contemporaries, made no more appeal to Nicholas than to Joseph Bonaparte during his Spanish sojourn. While Godoy failed to sell his Goyas, however, he did dispose of some thirty pictures, bought for the Hermitage for the sum of 567,935 francs by the dealer Lafontaine, among them the 'Martyrdom of St Stephen' (School of Pietro da Cortona); Ribera's 'Saint Jerome'; 'Three Saints at prayer' by Ribalta, and 'Christ before Caiaphas' by Gerard van Honthorst.

In 1832, the confiscation of Prince Sapiega's collection, in Grodno, brought to the Hermitage a 'Madonna' by Francia, and a 'Hunting scene' by Hackhaert. In 1834, the collection of General Gessler, Russian consul in Cadiz, brought in another twenty pictures and that of Paez de la Cadena, Spanish Ambassador to St Petersburg, a further fifty-one. Among the Gessler pictures must be mentioned a 'Saint Joseph' by Clemente de Torres, and among those acquired from Paez two Valdes Leals and a 'Saint John the Baptist' painted by Collantes in the style of Caravaggio. In 1836 a new agreement was signed with the banker Coesvelt, by which the Hermitage acquired for 23,400 *livres* seven pictures including the 'Holy Women at the Sepulchre' by Annibale Carracci and a 'Madonna' by Giulio Romano. Such minor purchases continuing from year to year soon acquired a routine character. In 1839, for instance, the Munich dealer Noé contributed, among other works, a 'Fornarina' by Giulio Romano and a 'Rest on the Flight into Egypt', attributed to Cariani. In 1845 the Russian Ambassador to Vienna, the High Chamberlain Tatichev, bequeathed his collection to the Emperor. Tatichev's collection contained some Flemish primitives which had so far been lacking in the Hermitage, including several magnificent examples: 'The Crucifixion' and 'The Last Judgment', two panels of the Van Eyck triptych now in the Metropolitan Museum in New York and two pictures by the Master of Flémalle: The 'Holy Trinity' and the 'Madonna by the Fireside' (p. 113). The Tatichev collection also provided the Hermitage with a 'Madonna' by Morales; a valuable late sixteenth-century copy of Leonardo's 'Last Supper'; an 'Entombment' by Francia; and a 'Holy Family' by Giulio Bugiardini.

At the Barberigo sale in Venice in 1850, the Russian consul bought five Titians, and one of his studio pictures: 'Christ carrying the Cross' (p. 274), 'The Virgin and Child', 'Mary Magdalene' (p. 103), 'Saint

Sebastian' (p. 274) and a 'Portrait of Pope Paul III', as well as a 'Portrait of a man' by Veronese, a 'Christ among the Doctors' from the school of Veronese, and a 'Madonna' by Palma Vecchio.

In the same year the new Curator of the Hermitage distinguished himself in The Hague, where he shared out with the representatives of the Louvre and of England the collection of William II of the Netherlands. For 173,823 florins he acquired thirty pictures, including the 'Annunciation' by Jan van Eyck, now in the National Gallery in Washington, a 'Coronation of the Virgin' then attributed to Van Orley, and 'Saint Luke painting the Virgin' (p. 115) by Rogier van der Weyden – the latter in reality a fragment of the picture in which this artist represented St Luke painting the portrait of the Virgin, a work reconstituted twenty-four years later when reunited in Strasbourg with the other main fragment.

On the Italian side, William's collection contributed a 'Descent from the Cross' by Sebastiano del Piombo; a 'Portrait of an old man' by Bacchiaca, then attributed to Raphael, the 'Martyrdom of St Catherine' by Guercino; 'The betrothed' by B. Van der Helst; a 'Joseph and the Child on the Flight into Egypt' by Guido Reni, and a very fine 'Portrait of a woman' by Melzi, reminiscent of certain figures by Leonardo.

In 1852, shortly after the accession of Napoleon III as Emperor, Bruni went to Paris where he attended the sale of the collection of Marshal Soult, who had died the previous year. He brought back a 'Christ carrying the Cross' (p. 275) by Sebastiano del Piombo, a dramatic work heralding El Greco fifty years before his time, and a 'Saint Lawrence' by Zurbaran (p. 289), showing the Saint, wearing a gold-embroidered chasuble, and holding in his hand the gridiron on which he met his martyrdom. From the duc de Morny's estate, Bruni bought for 8,000 francs Rembrandt's 'Portrait of an old man' (p. 284); from that of the Baroness d'Este he purchased 'The Virgin appearing to a Dominican Monk', a monumental work by Alonso Cano, while from the Laneuville collection he acquired yet another Murillo: 'The Vision of St Anthony'.

On February 5, 1852, after twelve years of work, the Hermitage was opened as a public museum with due ceremony by Nicholas I. In 1837 the Winter Palace had been ravaged by fire. Only the façades and a few of the rooms had remained standing. The interior had had to be entirely rebuilt. The architect Stassov had restored the little throne room, carefully preserving the original character given to it by the French architect Ricard de Montferrand. The only real change due to Bullov and Stassov was the mural decoration of gold, bronze, malachite and precious stones from the Urals, in the rooms designed by Rastrelli seventy-five years before. Nicholas decided to take the opportunity offered by this restoration to create a Museum.

In 1840 he brought from Munich the architect Leo von Klenze, who, together with the Russians Efimov and Stassov, designed the plans of the building later known as the New Hermitage. The work lasted nine years. In 1849, the Curators drew up a new inventory of the Emperor's 4,500 pictures. Bruni, with the assistance of P. Basin and T. Neef, at the same time carried out a difficult process of selection. They had to divide up the pictures between those worthy of exhibition, those of purely decorative interest, those to be sent to the reserves, and finally those of lesser value. Eight hundred and fifteen pictures were selected for the Museum, eight hundred and four remained in the reserves and one thousand, five hundred and sixty-one were rejected as being of minor interest.

There are several points of resemblance between the Pinakothek and Glyptothek in Munich (built some twenty years previously by Ludwig I), and the New Hermitage, installed in a building close to the Winter Palace. The explanation is not far to seek. The three buildings were all designed and executed by the same architect, Klenze, whose usual style, inspired by Roman palaces, resulted in a building both austere and highly decorated, its entrance a portico supported by ten gigantic Atlantes hewn out of Finnish granite by the Russian sculptor Terebenev.

On February 5, 1852, the public was invited to admire the exhibition and to pronounce judgment on the internal organization of the Museum. On the ground floor were the rooms containing classical sculpture, vases, bronzes and the 'Siberian antiquities'. On the first floor the paintings were grouped by schools, and not, as previously, according to purely decorative considerations. In 1898, a section devoted to Russian works was added to the foreign schools.

The selection effected by the Curators was inspired both by a desire not to crowd the walls, and by a decision to exhibit only works of major interest. They thus found themselves obliged to relegate many pictures to the reserves, and were constantly haunted by the fear of excluding some unrecognised masterpiece which, brought to light and subjected to reappraisal at some future date, might reopen the whole delicate problem of selection.

For museum curators as for art historians, the history of the past is a constant demonstration of the fluctuation of taste, a continuous story of neglect, followed by discovery or rediscovery.

In 1853, Nicholas I decided to sell 1219 pictures out of the total of the 4,552 contained in the collections as a whole; i. e. more than one picture in four. Among the most notable works thus dispersed were the panels of the triptych 'The Healing of the Blind Man of Jericho' (p. 279) by Lucas van Leyden, acquired by Catherine from the Crozat collection, happily rediscovered and repurchased by a St Petersburg collector thirty-three years later; a work by Lastman, the master of Rembrandt, which returned to the Hermitage only in 1938; the 'Attributes of the Arts' by Chardin (p. 173), and 'Cupid sharpening his Arrow' by Natoire (also previously in the Crozat collection) which reappeared on the Hermitage walls after the Revolution. The choice of the Curators had not been directed against any particular school or style of painting. Despite its impartiality, however, this 'axeing commission' severely harmed the Museum and only the nationalisation of private collections following the Revolution was able to mitigate, if not to eliminate, the results of certain arbitrary decisions.

Alexander II, liberator of the serfs and successor to Nicholas I, reigned from 1855 to 1881. He did not greatly concern himself with the Hermitage. The Museum was now an independent administration, managing its own affairs and—and this is not really surprising—deciding its own purchases and alterations. There was, indeed, plenty to be done in the way of organization. From 1856 to 1859 work was carried out on a new inventory and a new catalogue supervised by G. F. Waagen, Director of the Berlin Museum. Waagen introduced a more stringent order into the Hermitage, often reversing decisions reached by the Bruni commission ten years earlier – relegating to the cellars pictures which were on the walls and vice versa. His arrangements remained intact until the Revolution, and the catalogue of 1863, improved and rendered more explicit on the advice of Paul Lacroix and of Thoré Burger, remained the authoritative one until that published by A. Somov, continuing the work of Bruiningk.

The Museum was now deemed to have reached perfection. In Russia, as in the rest of Europe, museums were entering a period of stability, and for years on end their contents remained untouched: the pictures hanging on the same nails, the statues set on the same pedestals, the objets d'art protected inside the same glass cases. The art historians had won their first victory, and pictures were no longer arranged for visual pleasure but in accordance with a thorough knowledge of the works themselves.

During this period of organization, fewer works were bought than under Nicholas I. In 1861, the Russians, like the English, let the paintings collected by the Marquis of Campana, purchased by Napoleon III for the Louvre (which, however, did not keep them), slip through their fingers. The Russians were left with the collections of classical painted vases and of sculpture, as well as nine frescoes by the school of Raphael. Gheneonov, who negotiated these Roman purchases, was one of the best Curators ever in charge of the Hermitage. Five years later he acquired an exceptionally fine Da Vinci, purchasing from the Duke of Litta in Milan for the sum of 100,000 francs a Sassoferrato 'Madonna'; a 'Venus' by Lavinia Fontana; an 'Apollo and Mars' by the school of Parmigiano and Leonardo's famous 'Madonna Litta' (p. 87) which like the 'Mona Lisa' in the Louvre, is the most celebrated picture in the Hermitage.

Acquisitions no longer depended upon the Sovereign's choice, and the degree of interest manifested by successive rulers no longer affected the artistic development of the Hermitage. The incorporation of the Imperial collections into the national patrimony aroused no rivalry between the proprietors and those charged with the supervision, administration and eventual disposal of this property. Thus when Ghedeonov purchased from Count Conestabile in Perugia the celebrated Raphael 'Madonna Conestabile' (p. 93), it remained in the imperial residence for ten years before the Empress Maria Alexandrovna restored it to the Museum for which it had been destined.

The following year, the new Curator, Vasilchnikov, purchased in Florence, for 46,000 francs, a fresco designed by Fra Angelico for the Convent of San Domenico in Fiesole: 'The Virgin and Child with Saint Dominic and Saint Aquinas' (p. 83). He extracted from Alexander III (whose reign lasted from 1881 to 1894) some of the many pictures still decorating the imperial palaces. From Monplaisir (at Tsarskoye-Selo) came twenty-two pictures, including Rembrandt's 'David's Farewell to Jonathan' (p. 137), and 'The brawl' by Van Ostade. From Gatchina came works by Boucher and Tiepolo ('Maecenas presenting the Arts to Augustus', p. 108). This marked the beginning of a process by which the Hermitage became no longer a reserve from which the Tsars chose their palace decorations, but a central point towards which, sooner or later, all the great works found their way. In 1886, it was the turn of the Galitzin collection: seventy-three pictures were allotted to the Hermitage, a hundred and nine going to the Saratov Museum. From Moscow came in all two Rubens: a 'Virgin an Child' and a 'Jupiter and Juno', a sketch for the decoration of the Luxembourg Palace in Paris; the 'Annunciation' of Cima de Conegliano (p. 91); two 'Landscapes' by Joos de Momper; a 'Venice' by Guardi (p. 277); a 'Portrait of Louis XIV' by Van der Meulen and works by Wouwerman, Allori, Neefs, Savery, Berchem, etc. The century ended with the purchase of a number of pictures by Eeckhout, Eliasz, Claesz; a fine 'Landscape with figures' by Gillis van Coninxloo; a 'Saint Jerome' by Van Hemessen, a 'View of Venice' by Guardi and certain pictures from the Lesenki Palace in Warsaw, formerly the property of King Stanislaus-Augustus: Fragonard's 'Stolen kiss' (p. 177) and a 'Self-portrait' by Aert van Gelder. Meanwhile, the Russian works were transferred from the

Hermitage to the Russian Museum set up in the Mikhailovsky Palace in 1898.

Between 1910 and 1932 the Hermitage doubled the number of its pictures. No museum has ever grown at a more rapid pace: purchases, the nationalisation of private collections, and the reshuffling of public collections all contributed their share, while the Hermitage itself, at the centre of this general post of works of art, proceeded to donate, to exchange and to sell. It remained the focal point of the reorganization of Russian museums, and emerged from this momentous period as the greatest museum in the Soviet Union. The Soviets might well have chosen to give preference to Moscow, the capital. The Pushkin Museum was, indeed, considerably enriched, but the Hermitage remained pre-eminent. We have already seen that the total number of pictures given in the inventory made after the sale organized by Nicholas I in 1853 was 3,333. A century later the Hermitage collections comprised over 8,000 pictures, 40,000 drawings and 500,000 engravings.

How had such a prodigious collection of works of art been achieved? Certainly in a more rational manner than in previous years. It is difficult to imagine the Tsar, or the President of the USSR, studying the Paris Salons, ordering a picture from Picasso, outbidding with their roubles the dollars offered for private collections, or corresponding at length with a Swiss or Dutch art critic in hot pursuit of some rare specimen. A few decrees and contracts were all that was required. Henceforward the Hermitage benefitted only from Russian collections. Russia drew a line under the past, added up the total of the contents of all the private collections and transferred them to the public domain.

The first important purchase was that of the Semenov collection in 1910: its seven hundred pictures, mostly Dutch with a minority of French, classified and catalogued, entered the Hermitage five years later. They were not works of universal renown, but pictures by those 'petits maîtres' among whom men of taste and erudition are often able to discern great artists. Mention should be made of a picture by that rare artist Karel Fabritius: 'Ruth and Boaz'; works by Dirck Hals (brother of Frans), Govaert Flinck, and Nicolas Maes; two pictures by Lastman; two Brenckelenkams; a strange work by Esaias Boursse; still-life studies by Rijckhals and Kalf; two Honthorsts, including the 'Portrait of Wilhelm II, Prince of Orange', part of whose collection had been secured for the Hermitage in 1850; a 'Merchant' by Aertsen; landscapes by Savery and Van Goyen; a 'Cephalus and Procris' by Rombouts, as well as works by Van Ostade, Jan Steen and Teniers. The year 1912 brought another important acquisition: the Stroganov collection, initiated by Baron Alexander Stroganov (1738–1811) who, in spite of many years spent in Paris, acquired fewer French pictures than Italian, Dutch and Flemish works. The preface which he himself wrote to the catalogue of his collection (St Petersburg, 1880) expresses a passionate love of painting. 'From cold-hearted collectors and un-cultivated connoisseurs, Good Lord, deliver us,' was his cry. On his death his collection was split up. From Count Stroganov in Rome the Hermitage acquired a 'Reliquary' painted by Fra Angelico for the Convent of San Domenico in Fiesole; a late fourteenth-century Sienese picture, and the famous 'Virgin of the Annunciation' (p. 81) by Simone Martini. From Count Paul Stroganov, who remained in St Petersburg in the family palace designed by Rastrelli, the Hermitage subsequently obtained a 'St Andrew' by Domenichino, a 'Christ carrying the Cross' by Maineri and two Filippino Lippis: an 'Adoration of the Child' and an 'Annunciation'. In 1914, Benois, then Curator, acquired for the Hermitage the Da Vinci Madonna, subsequently known as the 'Benois Madonna', and Cambiaso's 'Venus and Cupid'. In 1915 were added works by Daniel Seghers, Claesz, Lépicié, Saxon, Codde, from the Zubov collection, and, in 1916, the Kitrov collection contributed a number of English works: a number of portraits by Lawrence ('Lady Raglan'), Romney, Raeburn, John Opie and Gainsborough ('The Duchess of Beaufort').

These unobtrusive acquisitions were but minor events compared with all the upheavals soon to come: the removal of the pictures to Moscow, and their subsequent return to Leningrad, all fortunately without incident. The Russian Revolution succeeded in avoiding that pillage and destruction that generally attends popular uprisings.

Moreover, scarcely had the revolutionaries seized power, than they declared all private collections to be the property of the nation. Few collectors had foreseen the fall of the Tsars. Except for part of the Stroganov collection, which had been despatched to Rome, and the Leuchtenberg pictures, everything was still in Russia. Although Russian collectors were known to have made important purchases during the preceding hundred and fifty years, the actual number of their masterpieces surpassed all expectations, countless treasures being brought to light after the Revolution.

In 1862, the Kuchelev-Bezborodko collection had been bequeathed to the St Petersburg Academy of Fine Arts. This comprised a miscellaneous assortment of pictures among which were a number of valuable works constituting the core of the Academy collection. Among works by famous artists were the astonishing 'The fair' attributed to Bruegel (p. 279), Jordaens' famous 'The Royal Banquet' (p. 281); a 'Christ' by Rubens, a 'Temptation of St Anthony' by Teniers; a 'Portrait' by Nicolas Maes; works by Van Ostade and Ter Borch, and a group of nineteenth-century works: Decamps, Delacroix ('Moroccan saddling his horse', p. 179) and the 'Lion-hunt in Morocco' (p. 295); Delaroche, Diaz, Daubigny, Dupré, Millet ('Women carrying firewood', p. 296); Troyen, Isabey, Courbet ('Landscape') and Corot ('Evening' and 'Morning'), not to mention the usual works by Greuze and Vernet and – much rarer – a Corneille de Lyon, all of which, after the Revolution, came into the Hermitage. There was some hesitation as to what was to be done with the Stroganov pictures: for some years they remained in the palace on the Nevsky Prospect, transformed into a Museum. Finally they, too, entered the Hermitage, constituting a really remarkable contribution. The French school included, as in all Russian collections, works by Hubert Robert and the Vernets (the entire dynasty from Carle to Horace, who was highly successful in St Petersburg), by Greuze, Vigée-Lebrun, as well as a fine Boullogne ('Lucretia'); a Watteau ('Caprice', p. 169); a

Henri Matisse: Portrait of the collector Schukin ▷

Lesueur, a Claude Lorrain ('Landscape with dancers'); two Poussins (a 'Bacchanalia' and a 'Rest on the Flight into Egypt', p. 161). From Italy came a 'Madonna' by Jacopo del Sellaio, an 'Allegory of the Arts' by Bernardo Strozzi, a 'Portrait' by Guido Reni, a 'Cupid' by Sodoma, a 'St Dominic' by Botticelli and an extremely fine 'Crucifixion' (p. 273) by Ugolino da Siena, as well as a number of Sienese and Florentine primitives to swell the meagre ranks of those acquired by the Hermitage in 1910. From England came a Reynolds ('Portrait of a girl'), an early work in which the joint influence of Rembrandt and of Rubens is still discernible. Paintings of the Dutch and Flemish schools included a 'Christ' by Albert Bouts, four Van Dycks, Rubens' 'Dejaneira', 'Landscape with horses' by A. Van de Velde, Hobbema's 'Forest', now very dark in tone, and works by Benson, Cuyp, Metsu, Van Ostade, Van der Helst, etc. The next intake was from the Shuvalov collection: several Hubert Roberts, a 'Christ' by Jordaens, a 'Raising of the Cross' by Rubens, a 'Portrait' by Lucas Cranach the Elder, and a 'Lute player' by Manfredi highly reminiscent of Caravaggio. The remainder went to the Pushkin Museum in Moscow, as did the better part of the Youssupov pictures.

Nicolas Youssupov, who had travelled with the Comte du Nord in 1782 and represented Russia for many years in Turin, had begun a very fine collection which was faithfully continued by his heirs, and, which, exceptionally enough, never suffered division. The Hermitage kept the Hubert Roberts, the only David ('Sappho and Phaon'), a Greuze, a Lancret, works by La Hyre, le Prince, Restout, Carl Vanloo, Boilly, Delaroche, Demarne, Pierre Guérin, Corot ('Pool in the forest', p. 295) and, close together in the Hermitage as in life, Fragonard and Marguérite Gérard. Thus, thanks to the Kuchelev-Bezborodko and Youssupov collections, the Hermitage acquired a fine assembly of nineteenth-century French painting. Disliked by the Tsars, it had fortunately appealed to the Boyars, who thus contributed to the treasures of the Hermitage. The Youssupov collection also yielded a number of Italian and Dutch paintings; two Teniers, a 'Self-portrait' by Aert van Gelder, a curious scene of the end of a musical repast in a courtyard at the bottom of a garden by Esaias

Van de Velde, a 'Tavern scene' by Cornelius Troost, the Dutch Guardi, as well as an Alessandro Longhi and an admirable 'Portrait' by Lorenzo Lotto (p. 274) depicting a richly dressed woman holding a cup, set against a landscape which stretches far into the distance. The Oliv collection contributed, besides some Hubert Roberts, a 'Portrait' by Laurent Fauchier, a 'Landscape' by Boucher (p. 293), a 'Portrait of Jellyotte, the Singer' by Louis Tocqué, and a 'View of the Island of San Michele near Murano' by Canaletto.

Thus, one by one, the great aristocratic collections came to swell the remarkable assembly already contained in the Hermitage. The enthusiasm of the curators is easy to imagine. From the Sheremetiev Palace came several works by Boilly; a Demarne; a Diaz; a Vigée-Lebrun; a Charles Jacque; a 'Holy Ghost' by Poussin; a 'Shepherdess' by Siberechts, and a 'Biblical scene' by Jan Pynas, a living demonstration to admirers of Rembrandt of the resemblances as well as of the differences between this artist and his master. The Durnovo Palace contributed 'Saint Peter and Saint Paul' (p. 145) – the only El Greco in the Hermitage; a 'Mountain landscape' bathed in glorious sunshine by Kerstian de Keuninck; an 'Infant Jesus' by Gerard van Honthorst; a 'Portrait of a woman' by Nattier, and a Greuze. From the Dolgoruki Palace came a 'Still-life with a pipe' by Pieter Claes; a 'Christ' by Borgognone; two tortured landscapes by Magnasco, and 'The concert', a masterly work by Hendrik Terbrugghen (p. 282). From the three-dimensional forms of this picture, painted in muted tones and softened by the pervading candlelight, emanates an impression of profound serenity, making it an outstandingly successful example of what is known as 'Dutch Caravaggism', the Dutch character, in this case, dominating the influence of Caravaggio. The Narishkin Palace contributed a Casanova; a Delaroche; some Hubert Roberts and some Greuzes; a Millet 'Landscape'; a 'Saint John' by the school of Tintoretto and a 'Portrait of Count Gouriev' (p. 295), a Russian Ambassador to Italy, painted by Ingres in Florence in 1821. The Maitlev collection contributed a number of French pictures, and that of the Mordinovs a 'Madonna' by Pontormo; as well as a 'Crucifixion' by Ugolino Lorenzetti from the Gagarin collection, there was a

'Vanitas' by Barthel Bruyn and a 'Vision of St Augustine' by Filippo Lippi, both from the Oldenburg collection. From the Kochubais came a 'Christ the King' attributed to Juan de Juanes; a 'Portrait of a woman' by Lorenzo Costa and a 'Madonna' by Cima de Conegliano.

The abundance of these treasures, too numerous to allow us here to do more than list the most important, were united on the Hermitage walls with all those removed from the former imperial residences at Pavlovsk, Peterhof and Gatchina. These numbered works by Van Ostade, Lambert Lombard, Van Goyen, Van Beyeren, Rubens ('Susanna and the Elders', p. 279), Mathieu Le Nain ('Portrait of a young nobleman', his hand resting on a skull); Oudry, Simon Vouet ('Veronica', the blue bows on the dress illuminating the picture and contrasting with the mysterious landscape in the background); a Titian ('The Flight into Egypt') in which we see the influence of Giorgione on the early works of this artist; a 'Madonna' by Alvise Vivarini; the 'Conversion of Saint Paul' (p. 276) by Veronese; a 'Flight into Egypt' attributed to Patenir; a 'Landscape' by Guardi; a 'St John the Baptist' by Luca Giordano, a Guiseppe-Maria Crespi and two Pittonis. These by no means exhaust the list and are quoted only to convey some idea of the diversity and richness of the pictures previously hanging in the imperial palaces.

The Hermitage was obliged to expand. Originally conceived as an annex of the Winter Palace, it now annexed in its turn the residence of the Tsars. Even this did not provide space enough to exhibit the rapidly increasing treasure (from the Stieglitz Museum, for example, came another five great scenes from Roman history by Tiepolo) and to study the pictures in process of exchange, sale or loan. The enormous labour of registering, listing and classifying involved the frequent displacement of pictures inside Russia, since a serious attempt was being made to establish a balance, to hang together what should be hung together and to divide what should be divided. The wealth of their collection seemed to the Soviet Government so fabulous that they proceeded to do exactly as Nicholas I had done, to offer for sale a part of their collections.

A number of public sales were organized. There were also certain private transactions with collectors such as the American Senator Mellon and the oil magnate Gulbenkian, leading to the export of those pictures now hanging in the Gulbenkian Foundation's Museum in Lisbon (Rembrandt's 'Pallas' and the 'Portrait of and old man', p. 284, Rubens' 'Portrait of Helène Fourment'; two 'Landscapes' by Hubert Robert; an 'Annunciation' by Dirck Bouts, and several Guardis); in the Metropolitan Museum in New York (Van Eyck's 'Crucifixion' and 'Last Judgment'); in the National Gallery in Washington (Van Eyck's 'Annunciation'; Rembrandt's 'Portrait of a Pole'; Watteau's 'Le Mezzetin'; or in Melbourne (Tiepolo's 'Cleopatra's Banquet'), etc.

The main public sales took place in Berlin and in Leipzig. In the Richard Lepke Gallery in Berlin on November 6, 1928, the saleslist consisted of: 110 pieces of furniture, 102 objects in gilt bronze, ten pieces of tapestry, some 40 snuff-boxes, 47 enamels, 36 pieces of sculpture, including some Houdons and some Lemoynes, and 97 pictures, including works by Bellotto, Benson, Bassano, Boucher, Canaletto, Cima de Conegliano, Van Goyen, Jordaens, Lemoyne, Carle Vanloo, Maes, Natoire, Netscher, Hubert Robert, Rubens, Tintoretto, Teniers and Joseph Vernet. On June 5, 1928, at the same Gallery, 109 pictures were sold by public auction. Most of them were Dutch or Flemish works (Van Goyen, Asselyn, Lambrechts, Paul de Vos, A. van de Velde, Metsu, Joos van Cleve, Rembrandt, Teniers, Swerts, Bloemaert, Gossaert, Rubens, Netscher) but the sale included also works by Greuze, Vernet, Hubert Robert, Cranach, Bassano, Guardi, Canaletto, Lotto, Titian, Duplessis, Tosqué, Giordano, Boucher and Bassani. At the same time some hundred pieces of furniture were sold, together with 129 items of sculpture, tapestries, Chinese porcelains etc. In 1930 and 1931 at Böhmers, in Leipzig, many engravings were offered for sale by the Soviet Government. On May 8, 1930, about 2,000 engravings were sold, including some 100 Dürers and 40 Rembrandts. The following day a number of Goya prints were sold off as part of a lot of 200 engravings. The sale was resumed on November 13, 1930, with the loss of nearly 200 Rembrandts (one of which fetched 30,000 marks) and over 50 Dürers, the major prizes in a

72

catalogue of 1,426 items. Finally, on April 28 of the following year, another thousand engravings, including both Dürers and Rembrandts, were also sold.

On May 4, 1932, the Soviets offered on the international market through the same Leipzig dealer, drawings including works by Boucher, Fragonard, Gillot, Gravelot, Greuze, Lawrence, Lesueur, the two Moreaus, Natoire, Oudry, Rigaud, Gabriel de Saint-Aubin, Altdorfer, Urs Graf, Cranach and Dürer.

No doubt the commissions entrusted with the choice of works for sale found it as difficult to reach decisions as had the one which prepared the sale of Nicholas I. It is also obvious that these public sales deprived the Hermitage of certain vital works, such as those of the brothers Van Eyck, now completely absent from a collection already conspicuously lacking in primitives.

Nevertheless, in spite of what we are inclined to regard as savage cuts, the Department of Prints at the Hermitage still boasts a total of 500,000 engravings, and the Department of Drawings has retained its 800 Jacques Callots, a Leonardo (unhappy seriously damaged) and two Dürers.

One cannot really compare the Hermitage with the museums of France, Belgium, Holland, England, Germany, Spain and Italy, all of which could find on their own doorsteps, in the studios, the churches, the town halls, or the houses of local private collectors, the basic elements of their great collections. The Hermitage was forced to go abroad, and to overcome many barriers—both linguistic and chauvinistic—in order to assemble so extraordinary a collection. Nor was Russian sensitivity always attuned to that of Western artists or ready to accept works illustrating the customs of such remote and alien countries.

An outstanding example of unerring taste, of true artistic understanding, is shown by two men whose names recur again and again in the pages of the Hermitage catalogue: Serge Schukin and Ivan Morosov. Thanks to these two the Hermitage, together with the Pushkin Museum in Moscow, must be ranked among the richest in the world in respect of Impressionist art, and certainly the richest in modern painting. Over a period of some fifteen years Schukin and Morosov each brought together an exceptionally fine collection of French painting. Both of them left enduring memories in the studios of Parisian artists, and the publication of the letters they exchanged with the artists with whom they were in contact is greatly to be desired, for they would provide a vital account of the 'heroic' period of Fauvism and Cubism. (Letters from Schukin belonging to Henri Matisse have already been published by A. Barr.)

Like Schukin and Catherine II, Ivan Morosov not only purchased pictures but also commissioned them. In 1909, he received in Moscow eleven decorative panels, painted expressly for him by Maurice Denis. In 1911, he ordered from Bonnard two immense pictures each over twelve feet high, on the theme of the Mediterranean. His favourite artist seems to have been Cézanne, from whom he purchased 18 pictures. He also had a particular predilection for the Impressionists and their immediate successors. The Hermitage now possesses seven Valtats, ten Bonnards, eight Gauguins, four Marquets, four Manets, six Matisses, one Jean Puy, three Renoirs, seven Cézannes, one Seyssand, one Signac, two Sisleys, one Herbin, one Van Gogh and four works by Otto Friesz, deriving from his collection.

Schukin's taste was more audacious. Fernande Olivier has given a somewhat unflattering portrait of this collector in her book on Picasso: 'One day Matisse brought to Picasso a M. Schukin, an important Jewish collector from Moscow, and a very rich connoisseur of modern art. He was a sallow, pale-faced man with a large pig-like head. He stuttered horribly and had difficulty in making himself understood, which caused embarrassment and increased the impression of physical weakness. Picasso's methods proved a revelation to him. He bought two pictures at what was a high price for the time, and proved to be a fastidious collector.'

This portrait needs elaboration. Daniel Henry Kahnweiler tells us that Schukin was not a Jew, belonging, on the contrary, to the 'Old Believers'. As for his ugliness, we may perhaps form an opinion from the 'Portrait' painted by Matisse in 1912. 'Schukin', so Kahnweiler tells us, 'was then almost the only important collector of avant-garde art. He liked big pictures. Whenever I had a group of Picassos I sent him a telegram, and he would set off at once from Moscow.' Schukin was then the owner of the Trubetzkoi Palace, and he covered its walls with works of art then considered highly advanced: Puvis de Chavannes, Whistler and Carrière. He was one of the first to appreciate Cézanne and Gauguin. When Schukin first came to France the Impressionists already had their place in all major collections and it was therefore normal that he should buy six Renoirs. But Cézanne, Gauguin and Van Gogh were quite another story! His admiration for these artists proved how open was his mind. Schukin next discovered Matisse and unhesitatingly destroyed the imposing decoration in his house, and commissioned a new one from this painter (1908). The result was 'The dessert' which when he first saw it was a 'Harmony in blue', but which Matisse subsequently dispatched to him as a 'Harmony in red'. Schukin showed no disappointment, and in the following year he commissioned from Matisse two new panels for his palace: 'The Dance' and 'Music' (pp. 249, 248), for which he paid the high price of 25,000 francs. This sum proves that Schukin did not pursue the policy practised by the majority of collectors who buy the works of new artists only at very low prices. Schukin must have been amused at the thought that a picture commissioned by him for his own house should cause such a sensation at the *Salon d'Automne*. He may even have experienced the same delight as that felt by Catherine the Great when the lintel picture she had commissioned from Chardin proved to be a subject of curiosity at the Salon of the day. It should also be noted that he never refused to follow the development of any given artist, even when this disconcerted the majority of the public. From Picasso he thus bought both Blue Period and Cubist pictures, although this crucial change in the artist's style was not endorsed by many collectors, including Ambroise Vollard.

It is thanks to Schukin's perseverance and keen judgment that the Pushkin Museum and the Hermitage can exhibit works illustrating every phase of Picasso's evolution, during the years from 1900 to 1914, so fertile in discoveries and experiments of every kind. The two museums also bear witness to the experiments undertaken by

Matisse during the same period and it is touching to see young Russian students on the top floor of the Hermitage deep in discussion before a Matisse such as the 'Painter's family' of 1911 (p. 304) or a Cubist still-life by Picasso, such as 'Violin and glass' of 1913 (p. 269). For this, too, we must thank Schukin, who dared to treat as masters those artists still regarded as suspect by the officials of the *Beaux Art*. There can be no doubt that modern French painting, no less than the Soviet Museums, owes a very considerable debt to this collection.

As a refugee in Paris after the Revolution, Serge Schukin could no longer afford to collect on the princely scale of his Moscow days. Nevertheless his home was always open to emigrés and he regularly visited the studios of his former protegés who, in the meantime, had become internationally famous. He was often asked if he did not miss his collection. He replied that it had always been his intention to bequeath it to a museum, and that, much as he would have liked to enjoy it a little longer, he was happy to know that his pictures were being treated with respect and made available to art lovers. His collection and that of Morosov were at one time in the Museum of Western Arts in Moscow. In 1948 both were divided between the Pushkin Museum and the Hermitage. The latter's debt to Schukin is three Cézannes, three Douanier Rousseaus, three Van Goghs, four Monets, six Gauguins, twenty-seven Matisses, thirty-one Picassos, twelve Derains and one Renoir, as well as works by Vuillard, Guillaumin, Maurice Denis, Van Donge, Cross, Le Fauconnier, Marie Laurencin, Manguin, Marquet, Pissarro, Jean Puy, Friesz and Herbin. Even that was not the cream of the Schukin collection, although no one can claim to know the work of Matisse without visiting those of his pictures that are in the Hermitage. The Museum also has some works by Fernand Léger, André Lhote and Survage, so that the *Ecole de Paris* can claim to be well represented on the banks of the Neva.

We have seen that the constant contacts between Paris and

Serov: Portrait of the collector Morosov ▷

LIVERPOOL COLLEGE OF ART

St Petersburg were to a large extent responsible for the constitution of the collections now on view in Soviet museums. Paris also provided a reflection, if not a synthesis, of all that was happening in the West, so that, thanks to the links established with the French capital, Russia was kept in touch with the main events in the world of art and of ideas. The result is that the Hermitage possesses many masterpieces which the kings and curators of countries further west proved unable or unwilling to acquire.

Re-organization of the private collections and throwing them open to the public has contributed greatly to spread the knowledge of art in Russia, and established the glory of the Hermitage, not only as a Museum, but also as a manifestation of a glorious past.

THE PLATES

SIMONE MARTINI (1283 ?–1344)   c. 1330
THE VIRGIN OF THE ANNUNCIATION   Tempera on wood
Catalogue No. 284   Height 30.5 cm. (12″)
                                                     Width 21.5 cm. (8¹/₂″)

Vasari, in his Life of Simone Martini, had no hesitation in identifying this painting as a portrait of Petrarch's Laura. Two of Petrarch's sonnets do indeed sing the praises of Simone Martini, but why should this be Laura? Doubtless because her name is enough to evoke that atmosphere of supreme intelligence and exquisite refinement, an admirable art of living which was soon to dominate Europe and to usher in by means of paintings, and of subtle poems couched in elaborate language, the widespread ascendancy of the gentler touch of France. The works of Giotto and of Duccio earlier on were both grave and tragic, powerful and moving. Simplicity was the keynote of their artistry, for their aim was to touch the hearts of the crowds which thronged the churches of Florence or Siena. Simone Martini, on the other hand, seems to have been working for an élite sensitive to more delicate harmonies of colour, more receptive to fantasy and to piquancy of detail, eager for a renewal of ideas in painting and ready to appreciate refinements of the greatest subtlety. In painting his frescoes for the churches of Assisi or Siena, Martini was no doubt still in search of arabesques and charm of colour, but post-Giotto painters (and Giotto was some 17 years his senior) could no longer paint figures which were not located in space, and justified by a clear if summary perspective. The aim was not realism, but the attainment of a higher degree of precision, lending weight to the figures, which were always far removed from the gaze of the worshippers.

Simone Martini's frescoes were painted in this newer style; but for his altarpieces (witness the two Annunciations in Antwerp and in Florence, as well as the listening Virgin in the present picture) he returned to the traditional golden background as though intending by its brilliance to enhance the bow-like tension of his outline. Only an initiated, cultured public could appreciate the audacity of this drawing, the boldness of the line of the hands emerging from the supple folds of the Madonna's robe, symbolic of some other-worldly elegance. No doubt their anatomy is correct, but the disposition of the folds and draperies belies the truth, composing a fugue with nature, of an ease and freedom recently renewed in the work of Henri Matisse. This is superlative art: look once more at the precision with which the haloed figure is integrated into the golden patterns of the frame. Giotto must, in comparision, have appeared a mere vulgarian.

Formerly Stroganov Collection.

THE VIRGIN AND CHILD WITH ST DOMINIC AND   Fresco
ST THOMAS AQUINAS   Height 196 cm. (77¹/₄")
Catalogue No. 253   Width 187 cm. (73³/₄")

'I am convinced', said Vasari, 'that his soul is now in heaven.' The life and works of Guido di Pietro – otherwise known as Fra Giovanni, the Dominican monk, and posthumously as Beato Angelico, are indeed of great nobility. It is always difficult not to be moved by the spectacle of a man who devotes his life to the fulfilment of an ideal. Historical research, while transferring Angelico from his place in the celestial school of painting to that of four-teenth- and fifteenth-century Florence, has done nothing to destroy his legend.

It is interesting to consider that, though a contemporary of Donatello and Ghiberti, Fra Angelico remained a total stranger to their art. He stayed deliberately close to Giotto (1266–1336), defending an art plastically de-termined by the rules governing the representation of religious themes. The sun is God's sun, the shadows are the shadows of Hell, and light stems only from the Saints. For Fra Angelico, art was above all a language in the service of faith. It would, however, be unfair to class him as a deliberate archaist. Such reversions are generally solitary, and Fra Angelico was by no means alone in his reservations over the advent of style and realism in art: no doubt the monumental sobriety of Masaccio (1401–1427) served to confirm him in his determination to resist fashion, and strengthened his resolve to restrict painting to the limits of the sermon. He seems, indeed, to have thought of his pictures in direct relationship to the public for whom they were intended. His altarpieces rely entirely on the appeal of gold and colour, on charm of landscape and delicacy of detail. The same visual effects appear in the decoration of the Chapel of Pope Nicolas V in the Vatican, but here our attention is further held by architectural detail and certain experiments in perspective. But in the frescoes which he painted for the monasteries of his order – San Domenico at Fiesole and San Marco in Florence – all gilded ornamentation is abandoned: Angelico sought no longer to charm but to inspire reflection. Hence this Virgin and other even more inward-looking figures. We are in the presence of the same inspiration as that of the great figures of the Byzantine mosaics, the same absolute sobriety of design, deliberately heavy but at the same time generating so extra-ordinary a sense of spiritual power that Piero della Francesca, though an artist always interested in plastic experiment, was later to revive something of their radiant impenetrability.

LEONARDO DA VINCI (1452–1519)　　　　　　　　c. 1478
THE BENOIS MADONNA　　　　　Oil on wood transferred on to canvas
Catalogue No. 2773　　　　　　　　　　　Height 49.5 cm. (19¹/₄")
　　　　　　　　　　　　　　　　　　　　Width 31.5 cm. (12¹/₄")

This may either be one of Da Vinci's earliest paintings or, on the contrary, come after the 'Annunciation' and the 'Portrait of a lady with the juniper tree'. Analysis is powerless before the mysteries of Leonardo. The originality of the talent displayed in this little Madonna is, however, more obvious than that shown in the 'Annunciation' which is, after all, a purely traditional work. The oil painting technique known as 'sfumato' was at this time entirely new in Italy and is here shown at its most enchanting. Moreover, this picture shows a vivacity, a spontaneity and freshness not found in Da Vinci's subsequent works. Leonardo's later pictures are charged with increasing numbers of signs and symbols, reaching heights of mystery undreamed-of in this little picture. The composition, however, already shows extreme complexity. Although, at first glance, a 'Seated Madonna' does not appear to offer much opportunity for invention, closer examination reveals that it contains no element which does not contribute to the extraordinary counterpoint of rhythm, matter, form and colour. Within the rigid framework of the classical quadrilateral integrity of the two figures we find a series of curves springing from the knot of draperies in the bottom left-hand corner of the picture. The Virgin's arm and the neckline of her robe repeat these curves, while a number of strong slanting lines cuts short any tendency to exaggerate undulation on the part of these dancing waves.

But this is only one aspect of this patiently constructed composition. It can also be seen as an alternation of light and dark circles. Moreover, in comparison with the 'Madonna Litta', it is easy to perceive the deliberate use of scintillation: not only in the folds of the robe, adding a series of brilliant flashes to the rich fugue of the composition, but also in the creased and dimpled flesh of the Child. In contrast to this dancing movement, we have the calm sky framed in the unexpected gap cut by the Gothic window, surprising scholars by the absence of the usual landscape. From whatever angle we regard it, this work is a striking contrast of movement and stability, of spontaneity and geometrical precision. Da Vinci had not yet achieved the great formal drama of the 'Virgin of the Rocks'. He was aiming at the utmost concentration of perfection. His contemporaries were well aware of the profound originality of this work: this Madonna was copied again and again, inspiring countless Italian and Dutch painters.

Formerly Benois Collection.

LEONARDO DA VINCI (1452–1519)   c. 1490
THE MADONNA LITTA   Tempera on wood transferred
Catalogue No. 249   on to canvas
                                         Height 42 cm. (16¹/₂″)
                                          Width 33 cm. (13″)

Here we have a complete contrast to the 'Benois Madonna': symmetry, rounded volumes, perfect forms, great smooth surfaces. Leonardo has here found his style, his human types and that serene, other-worldly atmosphere henceforward characteristic of his religious painting. In contrast to the movement of the Benois Madonna, this is a purely plastic composition. We have entered the world of statuary, where the flesh is no longer mortal, but lives to all eternity. It is idle to discuss whether this work is entirely Leonardo's or whether any of his pupils had a hand in it. The 'Madonna Litta' represents a turning-point in the artist's career and we may be sure that Leonardo was too sure of his own opinions, too self-confident ever to have allowed his disciples to take an initiative of which he did not approve. Just as the research director of a great laboratory allocates certain routine tasks to his students, so Leonardo may have allowed his followers to perform some of the simple copying. What matters with da Vinci, whose whole art is an art of dissimulation, is not so much the touch of the master as the concept concealed behind a technique designed to be as invisible as if the picture had no connection with the application of pulverized colour on to canvas. Unlike the 'Benois Madonna', this picture is not in oils, but in the old Italian tempera technique which excludes subtle gradation of light and shade. When dispute arose over the relative advantages of tempera and the Flemish oil-painting technique then beginning to spread to Italy, Leonardo, like Antonello da Messina and Giovanni Bellini, soon opted for the new technique. This, however, did not prevent his subsequent return to the old method which needed a clearer use of colour and a firmer line, as in this picture where the blue predominates over the ivory of the flesh, the red of the Madonna's gown and of the little bird's beak. The line itself is remarkably expressive. Note the boldness of the proportions of the left leg and foot of the Child, presaging Michelangelo, and adding an extra note of contrast between the Child's flesh and the ornamentation of the Virgin's garments. All in all, a strange picture, like all Leonardo's. Perhaps it is best defined as an essay in colour for colour's sake, unusual for a painter habitually far less vivid. Leonardo, however, was not a man to leave any path unexplored.

Formerly Litta Collection.

MILANESE SCHOOL (? MELZI, FRANCESCO, 1492/3–1570)   c. 1520
PORTRAIT OF A LADY   on to canvas
Catalogue No. 107   Height 76 cm. (30")
                                               Width 63 cm. (24³/₄")

Leonardo's artistic heirs are unexpectedly timorous, and it sometimes seems as if his pupils and admirers retained nothing more than the smile of the Mona Lisa. There is no attempt to carry on the boldness of the master's composition, the total harmony of light and shadow of his forms, the immense interior richness of his work. All that remains is the sweetness, the smile and a certain cold distinction.

This charming portrait, which has been called both Flora and Colombine, from the name of the flower at which the lady gazes, shows clearly that the artist (Melzi? or Luini?) admired only Leonardo's choice of human type. The dispersion of light among the greenery surrounding the young woman is something which would never have occurred to Leonardo. Nor would he ever have made so much of the monotonous but doubtless natural folds of the right sleeve of the lady's bodice. Da Vinci taught clarity and perfection. Here, disorder is the keynote, in spite of certain admirable pieces of painting like the left hand and the whiteness of the breast. Whilst the picture has a certain charm, it is basically no more than a pastiche painted for the benefit of collectors greedy for more of the original and yet ready to settle for something 'rather like Da Vinci, with the smile of Mona Lisa and the downcast eyes of St Anne'.

Let us now try to forget the obvious origins of this painting, closing our minds to the fact that this picture was probably a purely commercial response to a steady public demand, and, in the last resort, a plausible if synthetic substitute. The seductive quality of the picture is based on the contrast between the marmoreal purity of the bosom and the idea of a naked woman – a contrast rendered all the more striking by the quizzical look upon the lady's lips. Such contrasts often marked the works of Clouet, and were probably much appreciated by amateurs such as Francis I of France. The suggestion has indeed been made that the original of this picture may have been Demoiselle Babou de la Bourdaisière, one of the royal favourites.

Formerly of William II of the Netherlands.

CIMA DE CONEGLIANO (1459–1517/18) Oil and tempera on wood
THE ANNUNCIATION   transferred on to canvas
Catalogue No. 256   Height 136.5 cm. (53¹/₂″)
                                    Width 107 cm. (41¹/₈″)

Cima de Conegliano is typical of the painter living in a revolutionary period of art, who, refusing to shelter behind outworn formulas in an attempt to defend the values he sees threatened, adapts himself on the contrary to every twist and turn of the new ideas as soon as they are introduced, and whose work as a result is naturally somewhat heterogeneous. This explains the country scenes à la Giorgione, the upright gold-framed figures of his altarpieces, the Bellini-like Madonnas and the oriental studies in the manner of Carpaccio. His distant landscapes are as exquisite as his compositions are austere and monumental. He combined the pursuit of abstract beauty with a search for the utmost variety of visual expression. Indeed his art alone constitutes a kind of compendium of almost every tendency of contemporary art.

This very diversity demonstrates the rapid rhythm of aesthetic change in sixteenth-century Venice. There is a tendency nowadays to consider the breathless pace of changing fashion as especially characteristic of our own era, symptomatic of crisis, decadence and loss of power; yet, in the course of his career, Cima de Conegliano essayed as many new techniques as any modern painter passing from Impressionism to Cubism and Fauvism. For instance, the 'Annunciation' here reproduced, dated 1495, and signed on the piece of parchment pinned to the marquetry of the bed, marks a liberation from the style of his earlier paintings which were merely a continuation of the altarpieces of his master, Alvise Vivarini. Whereas the pictures he painted some two years earlier were mere figures stationed under some piece of architecture designed to exhibit his knowledge of perspective, the 'Annunciation' is already a major exercise in spatial construction. In order to convey an impression of depth in a picture composed of only two figures in an interior, Cima has employed a complex structure of horizontal planes. The eye is on the level of the chair seen between the Virgin and the Angel. The floor thus rises towards the horizon, while the prayer-desk on which the Madonna has placed her book, and, to an even greater extent, the canopy of the bed, appear to descend towards this same line, creating a lively interplay of surfaces receding towards a horizon hidden from us by the bed itself. This animated movement is set off by the peaceful landscape perceived through the window. Any hint of the laborious in this admirable picture is happily offset by the tenderness which pervades Cima's work.

RAPHAEL (1483–1520)   c. 1500
THE MADONNA CONESTABILE   Tempera on wood transferred
Catalogue No. 252   on to canvas
                                                      Height 17.5 cm. (7″)
                                                      Width 18 cm. (7¹/₈″)

Not so very long ago we were taught that art had its own particular hierarchy: the fine arts and the minor arts; civilized art and barbaric art, etc.
Today, all this has been demolished: archaeology, ethnology and the history
of art now constitute a single discipline. Great painters too were formerly
subject to a certain hierarchy, on the pinnacle of which stood Raphael. The
greatness of Michelangelo, the depth of Leonardo, all were eclipsed by
Raphael's beauty. Today, when beauty is no longer considered one and
indivisible, Raphael's niche in the history of Italian art is no higher than
that of the other great Renaissance painters.

The importance of the picture on the opposite page lies in the fact that
it is one of the earliest works of the young Raphael, who was then aged
about seventeen, before his departure for Florence. Raphael grew up in his
native Urbino, a tiny province, but one of vital importance in the history
of Italian art. Piero della Francesca, Jodocus of Ghent, Paolo Ucello and
Berruguete had all been drawn to the city by Federigo da Montefeltro who
died a year before the birth of Raphael, after founding there one of the
finest libraries of the age. Thus Raphael grew up in contact with this virile
art, acquiring from Perugino, in whose Urbino studio he had begun to work,
the qualities of delicacy and of elegance. Raphael learned his lesson well,
immediately surpassing the refinements of his master; elegance becomes a
state of grace, beauty supplants artifice. No detail of treatment enables us
to distinguish this little picture from the Umbrian Madonnas painted by
Perugino, and had we not been looking for a Raphael, we might well have
mistaken it for a particularly compassionate work of the Perugian master.
His influence on Raphael was long-lived. The settings of his compositions
were well suited to the younger painter, never a revolutionary at heart,
whose constant conviction was that art should aim at a subtlety so great
as to pass unperceived. The true quality of his painting, already perceptible
in this small picture – which seems a Virgin, but seen in dreams, not merely
set on canvas – is its unique naturalistic Raphaelesque beauty. Raphael's art
seems to spring naturally from some secret source – so much so that we
sometimes ask ourselves whether the keynote of his genius is not primarily
that of naïveté and of innocence itself.

Formerly Conestabile Collection.

PALMA VECCHIO (1480–1528)
PORTRAIT OF A MAN
Catalogue No. 2653

Oil on canvas
Height 135 cm. (53$^{1}/_{8}$″)
Width 170 cm. (67″)

The work of Palma Vecchio undoubtedly shows greater diversity than that of most of his contemporaries. It will perhaps help us to understand how he came to paint such apparently contradictory works if we picture him living in the world of today, witnessing the current ultra-rapid evolution of taste and participating personally in the contemporary artistic revolution. He was a follower of Giovanni Bellini (1430–1516), whose works epitomize fifty years of Venetian painting. Palma's works also show how much he appreciated the themes and transparencies of Giorgione, and the broad lines of Lorenzo Lotto, while his 'Adam and Eve' suggests that he was also an admirer of the engravings of Albrecht Dürer. Palma constantly reflects the work of others. His elusive personality does not, however, prevent him from being one of the most interesting painters of his century, mainly because we see in him the last outpost, the final echo of the Renaissance soon to be submerged by the wave of Venetian decorative artists: Titian, Tintoretto, Veronese. Palma considered his pictures not as compositions but as a series of figures. His mind was still obsessed by the golden background of the old altarpieces and, although substituting for their glitter the melancholy charm of landscape settings and painting his draperies far more freely than the highly disciplined Bellini, he remains on the near side of the barrier soon to be cleared by Titian. Palma's art was transitional: the future always apparent in his treatment of detail, the past still predominant in the over-all conception of his work.

His inability to accept the new conceptions in their entirety did not, however, prevent his trying out many of the new experiments. A comparative study of his concessions to modernity and of his reservations enables us to measure the importance of the revolution effected by Titian at this point. Palma's vacillation does not, however, constitute his only attraction. His country scenes show him to have been a great landscape painter, while his portraits – such as this man with a glove – are wholly admirable. The contrast of the gloved and the ungloved hand was popular with contemporary painters. Vecchio, however, seems to have been aiming at something less superficial than this contrast in his insistence on the curious shape of the material on which rests the young man's right thumb. We see in this work a highly disciplined study of the powerful lines of the clothing and the marmoreal perfection of the flesh. It is a muted portrait, whose colouring accentuates the model's clear yet restless features.

GIORGIONE (?) (1478 ?–1510)
THE VIRGIN AND CHILD
Catalogue No. 185

Oil on wood transferred
on to canvas
Height 44 cm. (17¼″)
Width 36.5 cm. (14″)

This picture is without doubt the work of a master. Only a great painter could thus have integrated his figures into the landscape, contrasting with the restless, pitted, chaotic scenery the gentleness of the face, the smoothness of the throat and the long folds of the Virgin's robe. The village in the hollow is the work of a superb landscape artist, who knew exactly where to place his highlights. A masterpiece – but was the master Giorgione?

Giorgione is a modern myth. Less than a dozen paintings can be attributed to him with any real degree of certainty. Even the date of his birth is uncertain, and although we know that he dominated the art of his day and exercised a lasting influence, his life remains for us an almost complete mystery. There are more paintings 'attributed to Giorgione' than there are Giorgiones. It is therefore scarcely surprising that these show such variety, such contradiction even, ranging from landscapes inspired by a sense of nature as a mysterious dramatic scene to grimacing portraits. A whole new style of painting has been fathered on Giorgione. Since, however, every spring contains the river flowing from it, there can be no risk of overrating the painter of the 'Enthroned Madonna' (Castelfranco), of 'The three philosophers' and 'The Tempest' (Vienna) or of 'Judith' (Leningrad), by imputing to him so vast an output or progeny. True Giorgiones are, however, not difficult to distinguish, though not by any mannerisms or stylistic detail. Just as the wine taster cannot explain exactly how he can identify a particular vintage Burgundy, so, to describe Giorgione, we must fall back on vague conceptions such as mystery or romanticism. Yet his pictures are undoubtedly drawn with great exactitude. It is, however, something quite different, the feeling of space, the contrast between abstraction and the quiver of a leaf, that makes his charm inimitable. Definite attribution is possible only when we find ourselves in the presence of this particular combination of perfect proportions with the utmost sensitivity. When it is impossible to counterbalance geometrical perfection with dreamlike emotion, then the picture is no Giorgione. In this picture it is the landscape that suggests the master's hand. But the face of the Virgin has a listlessness not attributable to his brush. Moreover, this is the work of an artist enamoured of colour itself, the very stuff of painting, its contrasts and its harmonies. Giorgione's perfect art was never at the mercy of such incidentals. Other names have been suggested, Cariani (c. 1480–1548) in particular.

TITIAN (between 1477 and 1487–1576)
Portrait of a Young Woman
Catalogue No. 71

between 1530 and 1540
Oil on canvas
Height 96 cm. (38″)
Width 75 cm. (29¹/₂″)

Naked, Titian's women always represent some Venus, Diana or Susanna, whereas clothed, they immediately belong to the community of Saints. A veil or a shawl covers the head of his Saints, whilst his Venus makes no effort to conceal the trouble she has taken to contrive the pearl-studded bows in her coiffure. Here, however, we have a piece of pure frivolity, a boudoir scene, undoubtedly something entirely new in Venetian painting. Two interpretations are permissible: either the handsome young woman was amusing herself by dressing up as a man, wrapping herself in a too-voluminous coat and donning her lover's feathered hat. Or else we may consider that the 'modistes' of the sixteenth-century were sufficiently modern in taste to think nothing of borrowing from contemporary cavaliers their handsome velvets and feathers. This piquant contrast is alleged to have been inspired by the naked ladies in their troopers' berets so beloved of Lucas Cranach. No need, however, for Cranach to put into the head of Titian's pretty model the notion of trying on one of the many costumes doubtless lying scattered round the studio. Her handsome figure is by no means unfamiliar to us. Titian also painted her in a fantastic formal costume, its full sleeves slashed with rich embroidery – the 'Bella' of the Pitti Palace. In the Uffizi she appears in all her glory as the 'Venus of Urbino', while in Vienna, though hatless, she has taken up much the same stance as in the Hermitage – the keynote being the contrast between fur and naked flesh. The appeal of this picture, the nonchalance and freedom which make it compare so favourably with contemporary German or Flemish nudes (Baldung Grien or Cranach, Gossaert or Van Cleve) lies in the casual gesture with which the model has flung the cloak around her.

There is nothing furtive about Titian. Beauty is for him an everyday phenomenon, which, while unfailing in its charm, is not in any way remarkable. This is a mature work, dating from the period when all the high and mighty in the land were begging him to paint their portrait or to supply them with some nude from his imagination. The painting of nudes came naturally to Titian, and whether we look at his 'Woman at her toilet' in the Louvre, the 'Flora' in Florence, the 'Venus' in Urbino or the nudes painted towards the end of his career, we find always the same type of female beauty to which Titian remained faithful all his life.

Formerly Crozat Collection.

98

TITIAN (between 1477 and 1487–1576)   c. 1553–54
Danaë   Oil on canvas
Catalogue No. 121   Height 118 cm. (46¹/₂")
                                                      Width 197 cm. (77¹/₂")

Michelangelo's verdict on Titian's Danaë has been recorded by Vasari.
'One day', he writes, 'Michelangelo and Vasari visited Titian at the Belvedere
in Rome and saw in his studio the picture on which he was then engaged –
a naked Danaë receiving the shower of gold. As is *de rigueur* in the presence
of the artist, they offered their hearty congratulations. As soon as they had
said farewell, however, Michelangelo, while praising its style and colouring,
remarked that it was a great pity that the Venetians did not devote more
attention to draughtsmanship and study. If Titian's application to the
lessons of art and draughtsmanship had been equal to his natural talents,
particularly in copying from life, no one could have done better or gone
further, for he had a fine mind and a brilliant, vivid style.'

The reasons prompting Michelangelo's criticism are not far to seek. Over
and above the traditional rivalry between Rome and Venice, and the fact
that the sensuality of Titian's nudes was bound to shock him, Michelangelo
was embarrassed by the artist's expressive use of colour. As sculptor, painter,
architect, all in one, Michelangelo possessed an abstract conception of art,
applicable at will to one or other of his different disciplines. It was therefore difficult for him to understand a pure painter such as Titian. No doubt
painters did not rank particularly highly with those who conceived the
Renaissance as a new humanism, a key-science to all the sciences. To modern
eyes, however, Titian seems to have revealed quite as much of the meaning
of life and of the universe as any of the master-builders, and in many ways
his method of expression strikes us as more direct. His treatment of the
theme of Danaë receiving the shower of gold is not as frivolous as one
might expect for so 'gallant' a theme, although the shower is represented
literally as a rain of golden pieces. Mindful of the fact that Jupiter himself
was the august and generous lover and that from his union with Danaë
was to spring Perseus, he has opted for a broad dramatic composition.
Mythology, however, was only an excuse. His real aim was to convey the
contrast of the bronzed, weather-beaten features of the servant with
Danaë's smooth white flesh. A thousand shafts of light shimmer round the
majesty of the outstretched body. Titian's nude is a nude of tragedy: the
miracle of a naked body causing the very heavens to open up and to rain
down a shower of gold – not a very glorious miracle in itself perhaps, but
certainly symbolic of Titian's love of mystery.

The 'Danaë' here reproduced is not the most beautiful version painted by Titian. The Prado 'Danaë', for instance, has a livelier rhythm and includes all the paraphernalia of the miracle: flashes in the heavens, light playing on the sheets and draperies, the figures illuminated in almost tragic vein. The Madrid picture bears all the marks of the date ascribed to it, round about 1553 or 1534, when Titian's work was gaining in freedom, his forms beginning to lose themselves in colour – the whole picture, and not the subject only. The present picture shows no trace of this evolution, although the naked body of Danaë herself is admirable. Other versions of this subject are to be found in the Museums of Naples and of Vienna.

Formerly Crozat Collection.

MARY MAGDALENE
Catalogue No. 117

c. 1560
Oil on canvas
Height 187 cm. (73¹/₂″)
Width 120 cm. (47¹/₄″)

Vasari had decided views about this picture too: 'In spite of its great beauty this figure, far from arousing any lascivious ideas, inspires in the attentive observer a deep feeling of compassion.' No doubt Vasari classified the 'Danaë' and the 'Mary Magdalene' among the Titians which he described thus: 'They are executed in such heavy brush strokes that from near to it is impossible to distinguish anything at all, while from a distance they appear quite perfect.' This reaction enables us to understand something of the surprise originally provoked by these pictures, towards which our modern taste is now inclined. Titian's later works are tragic poems of light and colour. In them we perceive the glimmer which heralds the approach of death, the dwindling hours of twilight, Beethoven's last quartets, the final works of Goya or El Greco. The painter has passed beyond reality: our imagination is struck by this symbolism and in this particular picture we observe with what despair the ageing artist has contrasted the skull beneath the book with the tip of the woman's breast beneath the veil – the whole scene half-drowned in the shadows of ever-returning night, symbolic of eternal darkness.

This 'Mary Magdalene' is only a first step in the invasion of art by a sense of man's despair. The Hermitage also possesses a Saint Sebastian, an even later work, which seems almost contemporaneous with the 'Martyre' of Debussy – the brilliant luminosity of the naked flesh transpierced by still quivering arrows. This liberation is fully apparent in Titian's two masterpieces 'The Flaying of Marsyas' (Kremsier) and 'Pietà' (Venice). It is instructive to compare to these late emotional outpourings the pictures he most admired when at the height of his career, the works of his friend Giorgione, who, some fifty years previously, he had regarded as the avant-garde of art.

As an old man, Titian outdid the audacity of his youth. He who had never desired to be anything other than a painter, attained in his old age a perfection in painting never before achieved by any artist; his colouring assumed a completely new significance, finding an expression as free as music. No artist before Titian had given so profound a meaning to the actual paint. No artist till El Greco entered so directly into the dialogue between man's soul and its creator, between man and his mystery.

Formerly Barbarigo Collection.

PELLEGRINO TIBALDI (1527–1596)

HOLY FAMILY WITH ST ELIZABETH   Oil on slate
Catalogue No. 128   Height 43.5 cm. (17")
                                                           Width 31 cm. (12")

It was for long fashionable to despise the mannerists, that is to say those artists more interested in the manner of their painting than in what they painted. Yet Leonardo insisted on art being a 'cosa mentale', and innumerable other artists have pointed out that a picture is after all made with paint and not with nature. Nevertheless, however abstract some of Leonardo's compositions may be, they can never be labelled mannerist. Mannerism consists in exploiting an idea to exhaustion. Thus with Parmigiano it took the form of a deliberate elongation of forms in the direction of elegance; with Pontormo, of absolute liberty of colour and of rhythm; with Beccafumi, of insistence on the contrast, albeit an arbitrary one, between light and shadow; and with Rosso Fiorentino, of near-cubist construction of volumes. Seeking a distinctive style, the mannerists often imagined they had discovered it in mere sleight of hand. Such particularization is now, of course, familiar to us. For fifty years we have been learning to recognize painters by their own individual harmonies and rhythms. A tricky exercise, since many artists change according to the extent to which they have been affected by the successive aesthetic waves of Fauvism, Cubism, Surrealism. Mannerist painters require a discriminating public, such as existed at the French court in the time of Francis I and Henry II, where the kings themselves set the standards of elegance and imported from Italy the latest fashionable pictures. These artists also needed an established social position, which is, as Lionello Venturi points out, why the first academies of art were created, that of Florence in 1563 and that of Rome in 1578.

Such an evolution is not, however, necessarily a form of decadence. It is an evolution like any other, and modern critics are right to restore these artists to their former greatness. They are no less admirable for belonging to a more demanding age. Such a painter was Pellegrino Tibaldi, a native of Milan who worked in Bologna, Rome, Ancona, Ferrara and Milan before leaving for Madrid where he died in the service of Philip II. The fact that his 'Holy Family' is located on the stage of a classical theatre is no doubt a reminder of the fact that he also worked as an architect. An almost surrealistic contrast is discernible in these figures, combining the elegance of Parmigiano with the vigorous forms of Michelangelo in a cloud-swept architectural setting. Mannerist and modern taste are never far apart.

Formerly Crozat Collection.

CARAVAGGIO (1573–1610)   c. 1595
THE LUTE PLAYER   Oil on canvas
Catalogue No. 45   Height 94 cm. (37")
                                                  Width 119 cm. (46³/₄")

Is the musician male or female? Where Berenson was inclined to see a girl,
Baglione identified the player as a youth. Such ambiguities are typical of
this artist, from whose works his contemporaries and historians have
drawn the most diverse conclusions. Thus, some sixty years after his death,
Bellori, his first biographer, defined him as a realist: 'He taught such
absolute subservience to the model', he wrote, 'that he never drew a stroke
that was not true to nature. He had no interest in anything but painting.
He alone faithfully imitated nature.' Bellori here calls 'realism' what the
nineteenth century re-christened 'naturalism'. Speaking of the followers of
Caravaggio, he says 'If they had to paint a suit of armour they were sure
to choose the rustiest available, if they had to paint a vase, they took
the ugliest and plainest possible. Their clothes were never draperies, but
stockings, trousers, berets. When they copied faces, their attention was
always riveted on wrinkles, misshapen chins, gnarled fingers and limbs
deformed by illness.'

Many historians, on the contrary, attribute to the influence of Caravaggio
all effects of contrast of light and shade after the beginning of the seventeenth century, exactly as though the devotees of chiaroscuro had forgotten
all about the 'baseness' of the master's subjects and regarded his pictures
exclusively as an interplay of light. It is true that Caravaggio is a living
example of the contrast of naturalism and abstraction: a truly remarkable
artist in whose works the momentary grimace alternates with the expression
of eternity itself. This portrait of a musician is an early work, to be placed
alongside his 'Bacchus', the 'Young man with a basket of fruit' and the
'Young man bitten by a lizard', in all of which the realism of the artist,
so strongly stressed by Bellori, is much in evidence. As in the last-named
painting and the 'Lute player' in Vaduz, the triangle of light which
traverses the top of this picture accentuates its composition, responding to
the slanting lines of the table and the bow of the viol and echoing the line
of the lute-pegs; it leads the picture into infinity while imposing on the
artist a geometrical design in contrast with the disorder of the fruit and
the unexpected vegetables near the score, as well as with the apparent
mobility of the moist eyes and the parted lips perhaps echoing the melody,
whilst the hands are gracefully poised upon the instrument. This is a musical
reverie, vaguely sentimental, expressed in a very subtle composition con-

sisting of a series of ovals of increasing size centred on the right hand of the player. Thus, like shadows on the surface of the water, these ever-expanding rhythms achieve a physical evocation of music thanks to which the crystalline purity of this picture, classified by experts as just one more 'genre painting', finally outclasses the endless stream of musicians adopted as a 'picturesque' artistic theme by painters from Giorgione and Titian onwards.

Formerly Giustiniani Collection.

G. B. TIEPOLO (1696–1770)
MAECENAS PRESENTING THE ARTS TO AUGUSTUS
Catalogue No. 4

c. 1745
Oil on canvas
Height 69.5 cm. (27¼″)
Width 89 cm. (35″)

With Tiepolo, architecture is an instrument of majesty. The colonnaded backdrop of this picture had already served for 'Cleopatra's banquet' (formerly in the Hermitage, now in Melbourne) and the staircase figures also in 'The Abnegation of Scipio' (Stockholm). This work was commissioned by Count Algarotti, himself an art patron as well as a friend of Tiepolo, in order to celebrate the new King of Poland, Augustus III (1733–1763). The figures may therefore be real portraits since Algarotti often bought pictures for rich foreigners.

Formerly Gatchina Collection.

ANTONIO CANALETTO (1697–1768)   c. 1740
RECEPTION OF A FRENCH AMBASSADOR TO VENICE   Oil on canvas
Catalogue No. 175   Height 181 cm. (71¼")
                                                     Width 259.5 cm. (102¼")

There is a tendency to think of Canaletto as no more than the painter of
Venetian 'Vedute'; the last large-scale painter of best-selling Venetian landscapes to possess both talent and skill. Certainly the Venetian tourist trade
is indebted to this artist, who gave the world a new concept of their city;
no longer Carpaccio's city of stone but a landscape of light and shadow,
playing alike on palaces and people. Venetian architecture becomes Venice
itself, shimmering in its coloured iridescence, foreshadowing the Impressionists. Canaletto as a historian and chronicler of his time has received far
less attention. Yet chronicler he was, continuing the tradition of Luca
Carlevaris and painting the Marriage of the Doge and the Adriatic as well
as the reception of various personalities of importance (in this instance the
Comte de Sergy, Ambassador of France) on the Riva dei Schiavoni.

In 1526 Johann Friedrich of Saxony, aged 23, married Sibylla von Cleve, aged 14. The Cranach family executed portraits of the bridal couple in paint and every conceivable form of engraving. The date 1526 inscribed on this picture led for a long time to the mistaken conclusion that the Hermitage was in possession of one of the pictures painted by Lucas Cranach the Elder on this occasion. This idea was supported by the fact that the young woman with the beringed fingers bore a strong resemblance to certain well-authenticated portraits of the Princess (notably that in the Weimar Museum). But it should not, on the other hand, be forgotten that Lucas Cranach found a ready market for his imaginary ladies, whether painted in the nude or robed in state apparel, sporting enormous hats and planted squarely in front of the inevitable landscape. For in such pictures the most official of all official painters, unremittingly at work in the service of the Electors of Saxony, their household, their army propaganda machine, was in fact giving free rein to his dream: an almond-eyed young woman, with lightly arched eyebrows, high forehead, her gestures as complex as those of a Cambodian dancer, laced into the curious and elegant lines of an armour-like costume of his own invention – a little minx with flesh as fine as marble, her diminutive fingers grown a little plump from too much leisure.

Few painters have sought, as Cranach did, to paint the perfect representation of their amorous desires. Cranach never tired of so doing, and this is perhaps his greatest merit, apart, of course, from the extraordinary pictures painted in his youth, painting of a faith and an enthusiasm which he was never able to regain. The metamorphosis of this ardent youth and pungent painter into the mature artist dissecting his passions in the interval between two court commissions with the precision of the surgeon delineating with his scalpel the shapes of life itself – this is a transformation quite as startling as if a Rouault were to become a Matisse.

296.

THE MASTER OF FLÉMALLE (late XIVth or early XVth century)
MADONNA BY THE FIRESIDE   Oil (?) on wood
Catalogue No. 442   Height 34 cm. (13½")
                                                       Width 24.5 cm. (9½")

No painter is more mysterious than the Master of Flémalle. Some regard him as Van der Weyden's master, others assume that his pictures were painted by Van der Weyden himself as a young man. Others again identify him with Robert Campin, another mysterious painter whose works are recorded in contemporary archives but whose painting is unknown. Some fifteen pictures, widely divergent in style, have been attributed to this artist. It is, however, not easy to see how the artist who painted this Madonna (one panel of a triptych of which the Hermitage possesses also a 'Trinity') could also have produced the meticulous portraits to be seen in the National Gallery and the gold-framed figures in the Städelsches Institut. Both this picture and the 'Trinity' are, however, perfectly consistent with the 'Saint Barbara' in the Prado and the 'Annunciation' recently transferred to America from the estate of the Comtesse de Mérode. We find the same concern with perspective, the same Cézanne-like construction, bringing out the flat planes – in this picture, the surface of the tray. This is not due to any lack of skill but to a deliberate attempt to solve the problem for which Van Eyck and Van der Weyden had found other solutions. A painter absorbed by this problem probably indulged in few other aesthetic adventures. Obsessed, like Cézanne, by vanishing points and volumes, his technique is very different. 'An orange, an apple, a round ball or a head always has a culminating point, the point nearest to our eye. The edges of the object recede always towards a central point situated on the line of horizon,' so wrote Cézanne. In the pictures of the Master of Flémalle the even distribution of all sources of light has resulted in a uniformly flat surface, pierced only by the 'lines of force' of the perspective. Note that in his pictures the windows are never fully open and the horizon is thus always partially concealed, as if the artist wished to keep the central point as secret and as sacred as the presiding Deity of these highly edifying scenes. But to describe him as the master of mystic perspective may be to underestimate the realism of his pictures. Probably this is the artist's own house: we recognize the same cloth, the same chimney, the same tiling, the same fire-dogs, even the same Virgin (his own wife?). The Master of Flémalle was a pioneer of the intimate in Flemish art, thus revealing yet another resemblance to Cézanne. Both were obsessed by the search for 'reality'.

112

ROGIER VAN DER WEYDEN (?1399–1464)   c. 1440
ST LUKE PAINTING THE VIRGIN   Oil on wood transferred
Catalogue No. 419   on to canvas
Height 102 cm. (40^1/$_2$")
Width 108.5 cm. (42^3/$_4$")

This picture must have been very famous in its day, for several different versions are extant, among them those in the Munich and Boston Art Museums. The Hermitage version has suffered badly. It was at one time divided into two pictures and, while St Luke and his model have now been reunited, the roof, the daïs, a window, some wooden beams and a number of details in the lateral woodwork are still missing. Regarded side by side, the pictures in these three museums appear identical, except for certain details in the tiling of the floor, in the right-hand window and in the related tenderness or dryness of the treatment. This work was commissioned by the Painters' Guild of Brussels in honour of St Luke, its patron, from the painter Rogier de la Pasture of Tournay, called in Flemish Rogier Van der Weyden. When this picture was painted, Jan van Eyck was nearing the end of his career. Everything pointed to Rogier as the master-painter of tomorrow. Already he had been appointed official painter to the City of Brussels.

Rogier's work is less precious than that of Van Eyck. We no longer find any trace of the forceful yet gentle aura emanating from the 'Marriage of Jan Arnolfini', the 'Annunciation' or the 'Seated Virgin'. Modern painting may be said to begin with Rogier: tragic as in his triptychs with their flamboyant Gothic gestures, or calm and almost austere when so required by the more stringent demands of his portraits. Rogier was no purist like Van Eyck. For him beauty lies no longer in the most beautiful possible application of paint. He was preparing the way for Expressionism.

This St Luke has often been compared to the 'Virgin and Child with Chancellor Rolin' by Jan van Eyck, a work which must have been almost contemporary, since both pictures show a Virgin and Child in the presence of another before a colonnade opening on to battlements overhanging a river. The conclusion is obvious: art is taking the place of prayer. Luke, the painter, takes the place of Rolin, the worshipper. It is tempting to see in the latter a self-portrait of Rogier himself, an amusing note at a time when paintings attributed to the Saint were actually being exhibited (Dürer speaks of them in his diary). The animal concealed under the reading desk on the right is a bull, the emblem of St Luke.

From the Collection of William III and of Isabella of Spain.

114

MASTER OF THE FEMALE HALF-LENGTHS (active c. 1530–1540)
THREE MUSICIANS   Oil on wood
Catalogue No. 435   Height 53 cm. (20³/₄")
                                                Width 37 cm. (14⁵/₈")

This artist remains a mystery. He has indeed been credited with everything too formal for Metsys, too delicate for Gossaert, too elegant for Van Scorel: he cannot be placed more precisely than in the first half of the sixteenth century and in Holland. Josse van Cleve is probably the artist with whom he has most in common. His personality is, however, completely original and the spatial arrangement of the three figures in this picture is the work of an extremely skilful master. A second version of this work in the Harrach Collection in Vienna appears both livelier and more complete; though not sufficiently so to warrant a decision as to which of the two works is a copy of the other. Musicology has, however, provided the key to this minor problem. In the Harrach version France Vernillat has pointed out that the ladies are playing and singing a court song, the music of which is by Claude de Sermigny (1490?–1562) and the words by Clement Marot (1496–1544):

Jouissance vous donneray
Mon Amy, et vous m'aimeray
Là où prétend votre espérance.
Vivante ne vous laisseray
Encore quand morte seray
L'esprit en aura souvenance.

This song was published in 1529 in Paris by Pierre Attaingnant (d. 1551–2). In the Harrach version the ladies are not using the original edition but a copy which includes neither the bars nor the tablature of the lute. The copyist has kept only the singer's score, transposing it from the first C-clef into the second, a perfectly routine transposition. This proves that the Master of the Female Half-lengths could read music and had taken the trouble to make a faithful copy of a fashionable song.

The Hermitage version, on the contrary, was painted by an artist who could read the words of Marot but not the music of Sermigny. Not only has he transposed it into the third key of C, but he has produced a purely arbitrary and unplayable version of the music. This is clearly visible in the singer's score, where notes and words are no longer harmonized. The conclusion is not hard to find: the Hermitage version is a copy. Far from rendering it any the less interesting, this serves to demonstrate the esteem in which in those days a work of this quality was held.

116

HUGO VAN DER GOES (d. 1482)   Oil on wood
THE DEPOSITION   Height 36 cm. (14¹/₄″)
Catalogue No. 4782   Width 30.2 cm. (12″)

Van der Goes has not yet achieved the extraordinary vigour of the Portinari
altarpiece or the gaunt lines of the 'Death of the Virgin' in which his
unique talent is successfully revealed. These later works are, however, latent
in this 'Deposition' – an admirable version of one of the panels of the
diptych at present in Vienna. On the reverse side of the Vienna version is
a Saint Genevieve, the second panel representing Original Sin. A youthful
work, no doubt, or rather one of the first works painted during the brief
career of Van der Goes, an Augustine monk of the Red Cloister at
Auderghem, near Brussels, who died insane in 1482, after what historians
believe to have been a bare fifteen years of active painting. An early work,
clearly, in comparison with the Portinari altarpiece, but one already revealing
preoccupations quite different from those of his predecessors, Van Eyck,
Rogier van der Weyden, Dirck Bouts and Petrus Christus.

Technically, we find here a certain freedom of treatment in the artist's
use of high points of light flashing in his colour, which is thus no longer a
bright varnish, but a vibrant, living matter, while from the point of view
of the composition, there can be no comparison with the deliberate sym-
metrical patterning of a painter such as Bouts. A bold initiative has here
placed in the centre of the picture only the mantle of the Virgin, thus
displacing the weight of the picture towards the top, emphasizing the fall,
the downward motion of the naked body. This is one of the earliest
Flemish works in which composition plays a role in the over-all expression
of the picture. The landscape too is important: no longer the traditional
Jerusalem hillside painted so often and so lovingly by a Rogier van der
Weyden, but a bare mountain top, a cross breaching a tragic storm-filled
sky, its symbol dominating the entire landscape. It is not difficult to see
why Van der Goes was the favourite painter of contemporary Italian art-
lovers settled in Holland or why it was to him the Portinari turned when
they decided to commission the painting of an altarpiece. Nevertheless, it is
by no means certain that the dramatic conception of this picture should be
attributed to any Italian influence. To Van der Goes himself should go the
full credit for having achieved the very real aesthetic revolution apparent
in this painting.

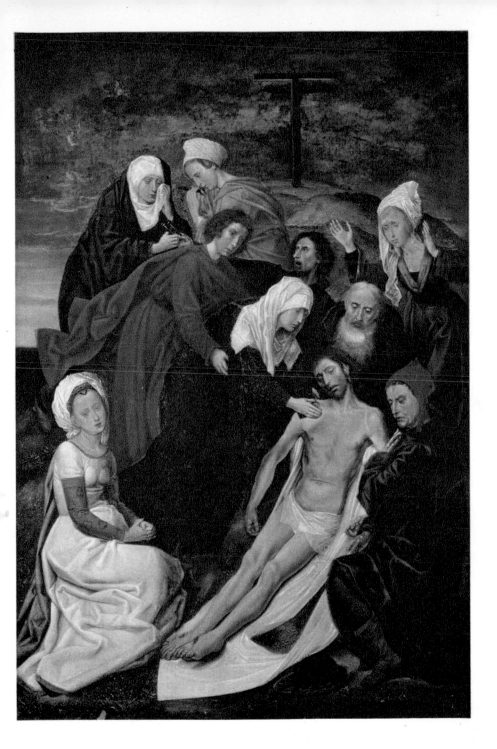

LUCAS VAN LEYDEN c. 1531
(1489 or 1494–1533)
Jacob Florisz van Montfort
(left panel)
Dirckgen van Lindenburgh
(right panel)
(Healing of the blind Woman
of Jericho)
Catalogue No. 407

Oil on wood transferred on
to canvas
Height 89 cm. (35¹/₈″)
Width 32.5 cm. (12³/₄″)

Lucas van Leyden, the infant pro-
digy and ebullient leader of Dutch
painting, is the archetype of the
artist whose work forms a transition between two different epochs.
His early works are contemporaneous with Hieronymus Bosch
and his last pictures with the early
works of Pieter Aertsen. In other
words, he witnessed both the end
of Gothic art and the birth of
Flemish realism. His place is at the
very centre of this revolution.
Whereas Gossaert was too much
imbued with the classical cult to
respond with more than a change of
subject, while making no alteration
in technique, Lucas van Leyden,
guided by the German painters, and
by Dürer in particular, envisaged
a complete re-evaluation of art.
He does not hesitate to launch
into the unknown, and it is probably to him that we owe the very
earliest 'genre' pictures in the
shape of his games of chess or

120

cards. A remarkable engraver, he did not easily acquire an understanding of colour: he always drew first and coloured afterwards, so that his pictures sometimes convey a motley effect which makes us realize how barbaric these new pictures must have seemed to contemporary Dutch collectors. The two Donors here reproduced are from the wings of a triptych painted shortly before his death, and the central panel of which is probably his most successful work. In it the painter achieved a remarkable synthesis of colour, light and form: before a vast landscape, already classical in its broadly rhythmic lines, he assembled some forty figures surrounding the person of Christ healing the widow of Jericho. The composition is still laborious but the details are admirably integrated.

In the stone niches, where formerly only saints might take their stance, are the two Donors, brandishing their coats of arms: the man in red with blue sleeves, the woman in blue, picked out with red. These figures are truly monumental in their proportions. The touch of caricature in the man's feathers is offset by the swirl of the woman's veils and ribbons. We are approaching the Baroque. Lucas van Leyden was without doubt the least skilful and the most inventive artist of his generation.

Formerly Crozat Collection.

121

PETER PAUL RUBENS (1577–1640) c. 1632–35
Landscape With a Rainbow Oil on wood transferred on to canvas
Catalogue No. 482 Height 86 cm. (34″)
Width 129 cm. (50³/₄″)

Four of five separate pictures could be made out of this one: Rubens
always bore in mind the example of Bruegel's landscapes, which he
collected, and wanted his own landscapes to be a world in themselves. With
anyone else the painting would be clumsily overcrowded, but thanks to
Rubens' ability to compose in terms both of rhythm and of light, everything
falls into place. The foreground is dominated by sweeping curves created by
the poses and gestures of the figures. Beyond this animated scene rises the
majestic rainbow: between it and the harmonious foreground we find an
interplay of light and shade reaching its climax in the ray of sunlight
which gives a mirage-like air to the bridge and the village. The highlights
point down towards the right, giving an impression of depth. It is no longer
a landscape which we see, but a universe.
   Formerly Bruhl Collection.

122

PETER PAUL RUBENS (1577–1640)
PERSEUS AND ANDROMEDA
Catalogue No. 461

Between 1612 and 1621
Oil on wood transferred on to canvas
Height 99.5 cm. (39^1/$_8$")
Width 139 cm. (54^3/$_4$")

Whilst both this painting and the preceding one must be ranked among
Rubens' greatest works, it has proved impossible for experts to agree upon
their date. This, however, is not unduly surprising, since Rubens was so
well satisfied with his own technique and its application that he did not
often see fit to alter it. He was too busy to have either time or inclination
to change. No general line of evolution is therefore visible in his work,
but rather a series of recurrent cycles in the course of which his ardour is
sometimes held in check, and sometimes given freer rein in the experiment-
ation of new ideas. Rubens is typical of the painter upon whom fortune
never ceased to smile and who proved himself exceptionally well able to
live up to its demands.

Formerly Bruhl Collection.

ANTHONY VAN DYCK (1599–1641)   c. 1620
SELF-PORTRAIT   Oil on canvas
Catalogue No. 548   Height 116 cm. (45⁵/₈″)
                                                Width 93.5 cm. (37″)

This picture raises a curious problem. In style it would seem to belong to the English period of Van Dyck's career. We know that after a long period in Italy (1621–1627) and five fruitful years in Antwerp, the artist proceeded to London, where he was appointed official painter to the Royal Court, and died in 1641. It was in London that he achieved that degree of nonchalance and ease, that noble grace and subtle harmony which were to remain characteristic of English painting for several hundred years. It has, indeed, been said that just as in Toledo, Theotocopoulos the Greek became more Spanish than the Spaniards, so, in London, Van Dyck the Dutchman became the father of English painting. This picture might be taken for a perfect sample of Van Dyck's London period. If, however, it is indeed a self-portrait, the youthful expression of the face would seem to preclude all possibility of its dating from the last eight years of his life.

The solution may well lie in the personality of Van Dyck, as Lassaigne has drawn it: the youth who never grew old, the smiling boy with clear (though somewhat black-ringed) eyes, fine nose, not always so easy-going as might be surmised from the numerous society portraits he has left us, the malicious expression of his face confirming our suspicion that his true intention, in painting side by side Anne Kirk and Anne Dalkeith, was to portray stupid self-satisfaction and self-satisfied stupidity. These moments of truth did not, however, prevent him from becoming the most popular portraitist of his day and the most brilliant of all the followers of Rubens.

In this self-portrait the elongation of the hands is no doubt due to the influence of Rubens, but, whereas the master sought merely to clarify and strengthen the line, the pupil is already in pursuit of style and elegance. We should not, however, make the mistake of thinking that the many folds formed by the coat just above the right hand are an affectation. This plethora of lightly brushed highlights and rhythms was composed to hide the fact that he could not paint his portrait before a mirror and at the same time paint his own right arm. But it is significant that he should have chosen to add still greater refinements to the picture, stressing even more what we might call the fashionable aspect of his painting. The brilliant pupil Van Dyck has, in fact, become the exact opposite of his master Rubens.

Formerly Crozat Collection.

This portrait dates from Hals' tranquil days. Much emphasis has been laid on the savagery of his last works, representing the Governors of the Haarlem Almshouse. These, however, were a cry of vengeance uttered by an old man over eighty who knew the worst depths of misery and for whom the future held no further fears.

Most of this artist's work was happy and indulgent in character and it is puzzling to see why the good burghers of Haarlem should have been so indifferent to him that he was forced to lead a bohemian existence almost all his life, dogged by bailiffs and pursued by creditors. But for Hals, the banquets of the Officers of the Arquebusiers of St George at once so comically solemn and so delightfully unconstrained, and the childlike good-nature of these debonair defenders of a newly-liberated land would be forgotten. Yet this painter, to whom they owe their place in art, was left to die in extreme poverty. His genius was not perhaps obvious: he showed nothing of that extravagance in which genius is often thought to find expression. The divers ways in which he handled his various subjects proves that talent can be clothed in many fashions. Like any ordinary artist, he painted banquets. Rustic 'genre' scenes enjoyed a certain popularity, so he painted these as well, introducing into his bourgeois pictures gipsies and vagabonds whom the purchaser would never have tolerated in flesh and blood, but whose presence, in art, was considered delightfully 'picturesque'. He painted portraits such as this one in which his sparing use of colour, far from excluding subtle harmonies, renders them all the more remarkable; the deep sadness of the eyes contrasts with the sensual, heavy, almost greedy mouth, and the nose suggests the musician or the gourmet. Frans Hals has also allowed himself one of those fanciful gestures in which some painters are said to take delight: the virtuoso touch of the crumpled glove held in the man's left hand, animated by a few streaks of light and assuming, in the darkness, the outlines of some tiny monster.

REMBRANDT (1606–1669)
THE OLD WARRIOR
Catalogue No. 756

c. 1626–30
Oil on wood
Height 36 cm. (14¹/₈")
Width 26 cm. (10¹/₄")

This is one of Rembrandt's early works. The artist, still in Leyden when it was painted, had already developed so strong a personality that he had gathered about him a group of young men, among whom were Lievens, a year younger than himself, and Gérard Dou, seven years his junior. This group met in his studio and painted the same models: old men from the almshouse and even members of their own families attired by Rembrandt in various curious garbs and painted on small canvases from every conceivable angle. These young men were drawn to Rembrandt's studio because it was the home of an art unfamiliar in a country where the rights of painters had received far less attention than their duties; they came to practise painting according to their fancy. This fancy was certainly Italian in origin, transmitted through Rembrandt's former teacher Pieter Lastman, himself descended from Caravaggio through Elsheimer. Yet the only thing Caravaggio and Rembrandt had in common was their love of shadow. Whereas the Italian painted on the grand scale, for the Dutchman expression came before size or beauty and his early compositions are as mysterious and secretive as those of Hieronymus Bosch. It is indeed Bosch and the German contemporaries of Dürer and Grünewald who are the real inspiration of Rembrandt's art. Faces watch the raising of Lazarus, bearded Jewish faces peer in at the windows of his biblical pictures. Rembrandt was already depicting a gaunt and haggard world, and this portrait of an old warrior (probably his father decked out in earrings for the occasion) is not untypical of the hallucinatory atmosphere of his early pictures. Later on, in Amsterdam, in 'The Anatomy lesson', in his commissioned portraits, we find order, calm and technical skill. At Leyden, at the age of twenty-three or twenty-four, Rembrandt was still expressing his haunted visions, either in compositions or in 'portraits' of himself and his own immediate circle. His self-portraits vary from the grimacing and the bestial to the noble and ethereal. For his mother, bent over her Bible, he had only tenderness. His father, the miller from the Rhine, was treated more cavalierly by his son; but though he often appears decked in turbans, plumed hats, or suits of armour, this frail yet ardent man, his eyes alight with passion, nevertheless touched Rembrandt's heart. It was a closed circle, but one whose fevered unrest was in striking contrast to the rich, solid bourgeois Dutch society of commerce.

Formerly Crozat Collection.

REMBRANDT (1606–1669)   1634
FLORA   Oil on canvas
Catalogue No. 732   Height 125 cm. (47¹/₂″)
                                                          Width 101 cm. (39³/₄″)

Rembrandt was married on July 10, 1634, and thereafter the figure of his
wife, Saskia, appears in dozens of his paintings. Do they resemble the model?
Rembrandt treated his young wife, no less than his parents, himself and
his sister Lisbeth, as a theme lending itself to endless variations. In one
picture he drapes her in a golden veil and gives her a Cranach hat; in
another she will be dressed–as here–as Flora. She appears full face, three-
quarter-face, and in profile; sometimes majestic, sometimes grimacing and
almost toothless; sometimes old and listless, sometimes, as in this picture, in
the first flush of youth. It is often hard to believe that it is always the same
woman, and it may be more reasonable to consider them not as portraits,
but as a series of characters played by his wife, a devoted model ever ready
to put on a disguise. This does not mean that Saskia was nothing more than
a mannequin: on the contrary she entered fully into Rembrandt's dreams
and fantasies. This picture shows her pregnant, holding in her hand a flower-
ed staff, a symbol of fertility. This was in 1634. Their first child was not,
however, born until December of the following year. Here Saskia represents
the Goddess of Fertility, her flowing hair covered by a typically Dutch
nosegay, including a tulip of which Bosschaert himself need not have been
ashamed. The setting of Rembrandt's mythology is not a smiling countryside inhabited by perfect creatures. His world is a haunted world where all
appearances are false and there is a second side to everything. How else can
we explain what is so loosely termed Rembrandt's 'eccentricity'?

As Charles Perussaux has pointed out, hidden monsters lurk in the folds
of his table-cloths and eyes peer out from beneath his draperies. Rembrandt
continues the grotesque tradition that runs from Hieronymus Bosch to James
Ensor. Here, between Flora and her leafy maypole, lies a mysterious figure
which may be merely an ornamental lion, its jaws open to spout a jet of
water, but which may equally well be interpreted as the legendary Beast
which terrorizes and seduces Beauty in the fairy story by Madame de Beau-
mont. Other shapes, other eyes appear in the dark shadows of the background. Flora's garden resembles the Garden of Armide, Medea's labyrinth,
or the sinister setting of Grünewald's leper. For Rembrandt, as for the late
medieval artists, contrast of form is as vital to the universe of art as is the
clash of principles.

Formerly Arentz Collection.

ABRAHAM'S SACRIFICE OF ISAAC   Oil on canvas
Catalogue No. 727   Height 193 cm. (76")
                                                    Width 133 cm. (52½")

This is the period when Rembrandt's skies are full of angels, when his women flee in full sail, when the air is cleft by crucifixes, and eagles spread their wings in flight: the era of animated, broadly rhythmic compositions. Italian influences are usually assumed, though Rembrandt never felt the urge to make the classical Italian tour. The picture market at Amsterdam was well organized. In the public auction rooms he saw so many master-pieces that his sketchbooks were soon filled with drawings after the Italian masters. No external influences, however, can fully explain so original a genius. The light, clearly articulated, rhythmic composition was, in any case, no more than an experiment with Rembrandt. He soon returned to his world of shadows animated by queer figures peering from the dark at the foot of his pictures, a darkness peopled with visions, a ghostly world of which Teniers was later to give an openly diabolical interpretation.

His first venture into this new field proves him already a master. Note the broken line expressing the interruption of Abraham's gesture, the only jagged break in a picture entirely built of curves. The angel's hand comes to cut the circle just as it is about to be closed by death: the dagger falls and the whole picture suddenly opens to reveal a vast, far-flung landscape between the great bulk of Abraham and the tender form of Isaac, painted with an intensity bordering on love. We cannot help but admire the stroke of genius by which the old man's hand seizes upon the head of Isaac, his great brown fist annihilating him as though the execution had already been accomplished: an admirable invention bringing new life to this kind of picture. Comparison of this Rembrandt with Caravaggio's rendering of the same subject (Uffizi) does not favour the Italian, whose Isaac is no more than a garish face effortlessly held down against the earth.

Rembrandt's landscape is fantastic: drawn not so much from nature as composed to fit the emotion of the picture, a topsy-turvy world in which the tree towers high above the valley, seeming to form part of the sky itself, and the surrounding sky, with its descending angel is not the same as that which lights the valley. The painter thus makes us feel that the natural and the supernatural, the human and divine, have met upon this mountain. The world has therefore two facets: on the one side the real and tangible, on the other, all that makes up the rest – and Rembrandt paints them both.

Originally in the Sir Robert Walpole Collection.

REMBRANDT (1606–1669)
Danaë
Catalogue No. 723

c. 1636
Oil on canvas
Height 185 cm. (73")
Width 203 cm. (79")

Scholars have asked themselves whether this picture represents Danaë awaiting the shower of gold, Sarah awaiting Tobias, or Leah awaiting Jacob. The question of its inspiration – whether biblical or mythological – is, however, entirely irrelevant to its beauty. After all, it surely also represents one of those glittering courtesans, whose hidden presence we may count upon behind the narrow, secretive windows and high façades of even a city as puritanical as Amsterdam. It is not difficult to identify her as such: the gilded cupid at the head of the bed is weeping and wringing his fettered hands, while the elderly, bearded creature drawing back the curtain with a bizarre, stunted arm, carries the keys to a remarkable number of chambers. A really dainty morsel, this Danaë, Leah or Saskia! What a picture of love, with those supple curves and soft volumes, that delicate skin!

A single note of contrast enhances the unity of the picture – the grimacing gilded cupid and the right-hand curtain suggestive of a tragic mask: these but serve to underline the unashamed, open sensuality of all the rest.

Nudes are rarities in Rembrandt's work, as in most Flemish pictures of his time: Bathsheba, Diana and Actaeon, Susanna bathing, a young woman in the river, a few Hendrickje boudoir scenes, and that is all. Protestantism, while encouraging artists to seek inspiration in the Bible, did not exactly recommend the choice of such voluptuous scenes, or of the Song of Songs. The scandal caused by this picture therefore comes as no surprise. Only in certain anatomical, cosmic, religious evocations of the Creation of Adam and Eve was nudity acceptable. But for Rembrandt human beings were always complex, difficult creatures, constantly in need of forgiveness, knowing not what they did. And what they did, moreover, was often most delectable. Rembrandt's portrayal of sin is indeed no more than a naked bosom glimpsed between two shifts. Bathsheba's nakedness is revealed only at the washing of her feet. Actaeon alone is responsible for our discovery of Diana, while the Danaë-Leah here reproduced is revealed thanks to the old procuress who draws aside the curtain. Rembrandt's nudes suggest secret rendez-vous and stolen glances; but not often does he show himself so violently enamoured. This period of his career is often labelled 'the return to Caravaggio'. This is a misstatement, for his use of light and shade has nothing to do with Caravaggio. We need only think of the dark Tintorettos, Bassanos, Beccafumis, and the Flemish night scenes of Gerard de St Jean.

In any case these resemblances are of no importance, for the beauty of
Rembrandt's pictures depends quite as much on his use of colour as on lighting.
His use of spotlights to light up his dramas is much less sensational than that
of Caravaggio: in Rembrandt's pictures the light, whether derived from a
window, an ascending angel, the last hours of summer twilight, hot, dusty
and pervasive, is always present in some form or another. Look at the
young woman's hand in this picture, transformed by the light into a sign
of welcome and of invitation. It is the focal point, just as is Samson's
cramped foot in the same painter's 'Blinding of Samson', where the composition is identical.

REMBRANDT (1606–1669)   1642
DAVID'S FAREWELL TO JONATHAN   Oil on wood
Catalogue No. 713   Height 73 cm. (28³/₄")
                                                     Width 61.5 cm. (20¹/₄")

Is this the reconciliation of David and Absalom, or David's farewell to
Jonathan? The city portrayed in the distance appears to be Jerusalem,
though the impression conveyed is of a stage setting, the city being draped
behind the figures like a painted backdrop behind actors. Altogether a
strange picture. Witness the contrasting costume of the heroes, apparently
of different times and countries, the fact that Jonathan bears the features
of Rembrandt and, last but not least, the extraordinary bleached effect of
the lighting. The composition thus appears as a kind of exercise in virtuosity, and just as Bach regarded his 'well-tempered Clavier' as a series of
exercises on certain notes for the use of young musicians, so it may be that
Rembrandt conceived this picture simply as a study in complementary tones,
or a chromatic variation. It is perhaps the most sober of all his works, or
at any rate, that with the fewest emotional elements. The composition is
austere – a single face, the figures standing in the centre of the picture, the
landscape suspended in the background. Everything is ordered so that the
eye shall not be distracted from the basic element of the picture: the subtlety
of its harmonies. The real interest of the painting lies in the ghostly outlines
of the mist rising over the city, the faintly-lit clouds and the light playing
on David's hair and garments. The work is executed in full brush technique,
and we seem to be in the presence of a gush of coloured lava, a constant
metamorphosis of matter into new and variegated forms and rhythms. The
slightest quiver of light on this stream brings to life the hair, or bows the
figure, anticipating Renoir. No artist had previously handled colour with
such boldness.

   Rembrandt was at this time plunged in many varied experiments, from
perfect chiaroscuro to the brilliance of this picture. At the same time he
was engaged in painting commissioned portraits and in the completion of
the famous 'Night Watch'. It was a fertile but terrible year for Rembrandt,
for June 14, 1642 was the date of Saskia's death, and it may well be that
it is for her that David weeps upon the breast of this Jonathan-cum-
Rembrandt.

REMBRANDT (1606–1669)　　　　　　　　　　　　　　1645
THE HOLY FAMILY　　　　　　　　　　　　　　Oil on canvas
Catalogue No. 741　　　　　　　　　　　　Height 117 cm. (46″)
　　　　　　　　　　　　　　　　　　　　　　Width 91 cm. (36″)

Rembrandt treated this subject on a number of occasions, locating his Holy Family always in the Holland of his day. The Virgin is dressed in the clothes of the local peasant women, and the houses are local houses. No other rendering of this theme has, however, such broad appeal as this. Often they are merely typical compositions in the style of the innumerable indoor peasant scenes of Flemish painting. Only in this picture has it been endowed with depth and meaning. The work rests on the meeting of two sources of light: one heavenly, the other earthly. The celestial light cascades down into the room bearing an avalanche of angels, a brush of wings, illuminating the face and Bible of the Virgin, and the cradle of the Child. The other light stems almost horizontally from the right, lighting up the carpenter at his bench, carving with his axe something resembling a yoke. A third source of light should not be neglected: the fire burning on the hearth beneath the chimney, its light reflected on the tripod and a handful of household utensils. This, however, is a mere detail, necessary to complete the balance of the picture.

The remarkable thing about this painting is that the partition effected by the two opposing lights in no way disturbs a unity solidly established in the form of a cross, its centre running through the Virgin's cap. The disposition of the forms, colours and high-lights corresponds exactly to the relationship between the characters. The luminous cross of the divine section corresponds to the half-tint cross of the terrestial portion, each complementing the other and giving the picture a quite exceptional unity.

The extreme economy of means should also be observed: the Child is shown only by a vague face and arm; the Mother by a tender look and outstretched arm; the father by a dim outline. The human element is thus treated with the greatest modesty – all the rest is a matter of tones, the red of the crib blanket, the more subdued tint of the Virgin's dress, the dull brown of Joseph's garments. The extraordinary blend of human and divine is achieved by the use of a constant progressive heightening or dimming of colour, creating an impression of depth. Many other similar analytical observations could be made: this is one of the most technically accomplished pictures ever painted, its great artistry concealed behind the humble façade of a Dutch interior.

Formerly Crozat Collection.

JACOB VAN RUISDAEL (1628/29–1682)   Oil on canvas
THE POOL IN THE FOREST   Height 72.5 cm. (28¹/₂″)
Catalogue No. 934   Width 99 cm. (39″)

In spite of much learned research, the life of Ruisdael remains obscure. It is
supposed that he first learned his art from his father Isaac and his uncle
Salomon. He is known to have died, unmarried, only five years later than
his father. We also know that some six years before his death he went to
Caen to take the degree of Doctor of Medicine. This late medical vocation
is perhaps the strangest episode in a strange career. His work, on the other
hand, followed an evolution admirable in its regularity. From the very first
he opted for the Rembrandt style of landscape: scenes in which trees, houses
and hillsides play the role of characters, and where the sun is handled like
a spotlight. Ruisdael can be regarded in two ways: as a man of remarkable
invention and a stage manager of extraordinary skill, or, alternatively,
simply as a realist. He is, in fact, both of these, capable of composing a
picture in response to an emotion inspired directly by nature, or in response
to an idea prompted by a work of art. This 'Pool in the forest', for instance,
is known to have been inspired by an engraving by Saedeler, itself inspired
in turn by one of Savery's landscapes. Most of the time, however, it is clear
that Ruisdael invented his own subjects.

Ruisdael accepted no bounds: like Bruegel or Hercule Seghers he composed landscapes aiming to convey a picture of nature itself rather than to
represent merely some particular natural scene. In the same picture we may
find a storm, a blue sky, a tranquil steeple and a raging torrent, just as one
of Rubens' landscapes in the Hermitage portrays both day and night con-
verging upon the same coaching road. But Ruisdael can also, when required,
restrict himself to a single 'natural scene' such as the 'Pool in the forest' here
reproduced. Though we are told that he met it first on a contemporary
engraving, it is possible that he would have seen it with less clarity had he
not, in 1650, travelled in the provinces of Guelders, Hanover and Westphalia,
where, as a true Dutchman, more used to urban than to rural landscapes, he
was struck by the wild, deserted, uninhabited nature of the country. But,
while his art undoubtedly underwent a change as from this moment, attain-
ing a deeper, almost tragic note, he never painted nature in the raw – the
nature from which the city dweller recoils in horror, fearing to soil his
clothes and sink his carriage wheels in mire. It is rather the essential tragedy
of nature that he seeks to show.

This picture inspires us with a feeling of death, a haunting fear of drown-
ing. Complete disorder, some trees already dead, others half-withered by

lightning, all gnarled and old, waiting only to crash into the watery gulf, suggest a stage in the slow cycle of birth and putrefaction. The distance, however, reveals a far-off clearing, and, as if to reassure us that the every-day world of men lies not far off, a farm-yard duck is shown fluttering back in its direction. A disquieting though subjugated landscape, seeming to crush the tiny passing figures with its weight. The actual colours of the picture are no more than hints. The picture is made entirely of thick colouring matter and of light.

141

PIETER DE HOOCH (1629–c. 1684)　　　　　　　c. 1660
Lady with her Servant　　　　　　　　　　　　Oil on canvas
Catalogue No. 943　　　　　　　　　　Height 53 cm. (120⅞")
　　　　　　　　　　　　　　　　　　　　Width 42 cm. (16½")

It is curious to reflect that Pieter de Hooch belongs to the same generation as Ruysdael. The absolute lack of any common factor between the two demonstrates the diversity of the taste of contemporary Dutch society, equally ready to adorn its walls with small, neat interiors or great, tragic landscapes, thereby suggesting that this bourgeois world was not the slave of any single fashion – and so all the closer to us and our present-day society. The advent of so careful, polished, highly finished a painter as Pieter de Hooch is none-the-less surprising. Naturally we must distinguish between Dutch and Flemish painting and remember the wide gap separating towns like Antwerp and Delft – Antwerp representing Catholic profusion, Delft (or Haarlem) Protestant austerity. History, however, shows that Antwerp, in the time of Rubens, was on the road to bankruptcy, while the austerity of the Dutch was in process of winning them a rich colonial empire.

To admirers of Rembrandt or Hals the work of a painter like De Hooch must have seemed extremely slight. Doubtless they found in him that concern for detail which they had learned to love in Gothic art, and liked to see their own simplicity portrayed with such a loving hand. This alone should have sufficed; yet it is doubtful whether, had Vermeer of Delft not demonstrated that such precision could be surpassed and made to comprise a multiplicity of light and life, we should ever have seen in this picture anything more than a charming incidental glimpse of a certain society at a certain point in history. Pieter de Hooch himself is typical of the oscillation of this particular style of painting between the pictorial and anecdotal. His stays in Delft (perhaps under the influence of Vermeer) inspired him to paint extremely sober work, such as the picture opposite, an elegant example of strong rhythm and skilled perspective in colours animated by the light. When in Amsterdam, however, he gave free rein to those smiles and other small compromises familiar to the artist seeking to beguile his public with some light and frivolous anecdote.

Formerly Lafontaine Collection.

EL GRECO (1541–1614)
Sᴛ Pᴇᴛᴇʀ ᴀɴᴅ Sᴛ Pᴀᴜʟ
Catalogue No. 390

1614
Oil on canvas
Height 121.5 cm. (47¹/₄")
Width 105 cm. (41¹/₄")

The discovery of the date 1614 on this picture astonishes El Greco experts who are otherwise inclined to date this work just after the 'Burial of Count Orgaz' (1586). In it we find the great baroque flourish of the flowing draperies as well as the nervous restraint of line which combines perfectly with the light to outline the figures, throwing them into extraordinary relief. It is totally different from the hallucinated visions of his later years, when light alone outlines the forms, and when stress is more apparent than logic. To feel sure of this we have only to set this picture side by side with the monumental 'Laocoon', thought to be one of El Greco's last compositions. In this late work the light is no longer shimmering but chaotic, unfurling itself in a quivering storm, at once diffuse and sharply contrasted, whereas in the picture of the two apostles it is so disciplined as to throw into relief the hand and bare forearm of St Paul as he leans upon the Bible. It would be surprising if, in the great inspirational period of his old age, El Greco had felt the urge to paint a work like this – exalted, yet as clear, as perfect, as logical as the proof of a geometrical theorem – unless he felt a sudden need to prove to himself or to others that he could still paint as he had done in the past. For in fact the date borne by the pictures is that of the year in which he died.

But this particular problem is less important than the tremendous vision and latitude of the picture as a whole. St Paul is the centre of attention; St Peter plays the role of the humble keeper of the gate. St Paul is the knight inspired by faith, with glowing eyes and iron fist. El Greco has invested him with a robe that is not so much a garment as a flame caught by the wind; a form created by the divine afflatus, hollowed out over his shoulder, making a strange sweep against his ears, while from the red cavern of his sleeve emerges that strong right hand which proclaims a world founded upon the Word of God. We can see here signs of the great freedom with which El Greco treats reality elsewhere in his work. He had no need to check with nature. 'Here lies the Greek', wrote Gongora, 'who taught Nature art, Art lore, Iris colour, Phoebus light and even Morpheus shade.'

Formerly Dournovo Collection.

FRANCISCO DE ZURBARAN (1598–1664)   c. 1660
THE VIRGIN MARY AS A CHILD   Oil on canvas
Catalogue No. 306   Height 73.5 cm. (29″)
Width 53.5 cm. (21″)

Who would have thought that the most austere of all the Spanish masters would have painted such a moving work towards the end of his life? We are told that his resentment at Murillo's growing triumph brought on the access of sentiment characteristic of his final pictures. He wanted to show that he too was capable of 'tender' painting.

Obviously, the artist who decorated the Cistercian monasteries of Jerez, Guadalupe, San Pablo, Las Cuevas, and La Merced, could not, in this portrait of a tender child, express the same nobility as that found in his stern rows of monks, or in the tragic 'St Luke painting Christ upon the Cross'. But he in no way belied the genius shown in these monumental works; were this so, then all his 'minor' paintings must also be dismissed, his still-lifes, his well-dressed saints carrying with equal equanimity a basket of fruit or the dish on which are laid the severed breasts, the blinded eyes which earned them a martyr's crown. In both we find the same self-discipline, the same triumph over the great pitfall of the Spaniard, virtuosity. Zurbaran is always accurate, perfect, precise, analytical and punctilious in his presentation of the truth. His world is a patient inventory in which object is laid against object, figure against figure, rather as the chess player sets out his pawns. Yet there is no need to fear monotony or the boredom bred of repetition: each element is so strong in itself that the only way, it seems, to integrate them in the picture is to align them in the simplest possible design. Another picture of the Virgin as a Child, of the same period (Metropolitan, New York) is even more eloquent of Zurbaran's disdain for everything that constitutes the charm of the Italian masters brought to Spain by Velasquez for the collection of his master Philip IV. In the child's room, the objects are placed neatly side by side: a pot, seven sparse flowers, a work basket a table and embroidery scissors. The Hermitage picture, on the contrary, consists of an isolated figure, though the brilliance and rich volumes of the dress and cushions fill the canvas with a vivid power. Zurbaran, a constructor of forms, an abstractor of volumes, was a painter after Cézanne's own heart. Economy and saturation were to him synonymous.

Formerly Coosvelt Collection.

DIEGO VELASQUEZ (1599–1660)   **1617**
THE DRINKERS   Oil on canvas
Catalogue No. 389   Height 167 cm. (64³/₄")
                                                           Width 101 cm. (39³/₄")

Dates of birth sometimes provide valuable pointers: the years immediately preceeding the death of Caravaggio saw the birth of a number of artists who, whether or not they owe a debt to the Italian master, undoubtedly shared with him, at least in youth, the same aesthetic considerations. This is true of Velasquez (1599), Jordaens (1593), Ribera (1591), Georges de la Tour (1593), Honthorst (1590), Terbrugghen (1588), Le Valentin (1594) and Louis Le Nain (1593). All of them painted humble people, strolling players, tavern drinkers and the like. Some investigated the dramatic contrast of light and shade; others sought only to convey faithfully the coarse, commonplace nature of their subjects. The young Velasquez was so enthralled by scenes of water-bearers, servant girls, musicians and drunkards that much later on, when painting such 'genre' scenes as his 'Triumph of Bacchus', for example (1629), we find him still faithful to the faces discovered in his youth. This painting takes us back twelve years to the time when the artist was just eighteen. In even earlier works, such as the 'Three Musicians' (Berlin) we recognize the same young stalwart (or perhaps a dwarf?) here seen brandishing the wine flask. The scene is Seville, where Velasquez, having left Herrerra's studio, had begun to work with Pacheco. Six years later he had already become an illustrious court painter, executing in sober blacks and subtle greys the official portraits of Philip IV. For the time being, his subject was this drinking scene.

The composition seems a trifle too deliberate, a little over-obvious in the repeated rhythms of flask and thumb, and in the almost playful emphasis given to what is still often taken to be a mysterious silhouette with lowered head, in the picture's dark background, but which on close examination proves to be no more than a cap and collar hung upon the wall. Nevertheless, there are already indications of a highly skilful, gay and vigorous artist. Ribera would no doubt have made these drinkers more disturbing, Le Nain poorer but more noble, La Tour more tragic, Honthorst even more tumultuous. Velasquez here reveals the well-balanced, generous, frankly optimistic temperament of one who found life to his taste and who was perhaps already more than a little in love with his future wife, the daughter of his master Pacheco.

There is another version of this painting in the Budapest Museum.

MURILLO (1618–1682)
Boy with a Dog
Catalogue No. 386

Oil on canvas
Height 77.5 cm. (30½")
Width 61.5 cm. (24¼")

The most irritating thing about this kind of picture is undoubtedly the success which it enjoys. Today's connoisseur rejects it precisely because he knows how many will love the little urchin's pretty ways, the pleasure inspired by the eternal freshness of the young scamp's engaging features and the insidious charm of his conversation with the dog. Stereotypes? Sentimentalism? Playing down to the public? Even the Dutch painters did not dare to display such charm. If, however, they are stereotypes, it was Murillo who invented them, and he cannot, in all justice, be held responsible for his successors. Let us then judge his painting strictly on its merits, in this and other pictures: beggar schildren scratching their fleas on street corners, or street urchins carrying baskets laden with fruit. The work itself is unassailable. A genuine realism bathed in the same gentle light as that pervading Murillo's pictures of the 'Assumption', characteristic of the tender rapture imagined by an uncomplicated mystic. What are the angels doing in his picture in the Louvre, while St Diego is in ecstasy? They are simply setting the table and cooking a meal. Even piety must have its homely side. Murillo was a pious man, whose piety ranged from tenderness towards dirty beggar boys to ecstasy in the face of ethereal 'Immaculate Conceptions'. The quality of his emotion does not change.

Such consistent amiability amazes us. But is was part of Murillo's character. His earliest works, such as 'St Diego giving alms', strike a somewhat rougher note, but he quickly acquired a sunny nature which remained unvaried throughout all the different experiments of his career: the sweeping compositions, the forms dissolving in light, and those ventures into near-satirical realism, jeering echoes of which rang out from Holland reaching even his peaceful Spanish circle. Broadly speaking, Murillo's fate has been the same as that of Raphael: after centuries of success, a sudden loss of prestige with the advent of a public which rejects what it considers insipid. Murillo, the sentimentalist, is himself the victim of an emotional revulsion. He should, however, in all justice, be granted an honourable place in the history of Spanish art.

Formerly Choiseul Collection.

PIERRE DUMOUSTIER THE ELDER?

(c. 1540–beginning of XVIIth century)
PORTRAIT OF AN UNKNOWN MAN
Catalogue No. 5743

Oil on canvas
Height 32 cm. (12½")
Width 19 cm. (7½")

This is a portrait of an unknown young man by an artist at whose name we can do no more than guess. Charles Sterling considers the vigour of its execution reminiscent of the drawings of Pierre Dumoustier the Elder in the Hermitage and the brushwork similar to that of certain unsigned full-length portraits in the Washington and Detroit Museums, attributable to the same artist. An ingenious argument this, which the discovery of further documentary evidence may well one day confirm. However this may be, it is an admirable and forceful portrait, certainly not the work of a mediocre hand. The picture's close edging (which may, however, merely be the result of a succession of cuts) almost suggests a modern work, as does the curious short-cropped hair which seems to grow in two distinct and different ways (though here again damage to the canvas and subsequent retouching may account for this). There is something modern about the treatment too. Sixteenth-century painters rarely revealed so clearly the secrets of their art. Here we can see precisely how the picture was painted and the light brushwork the artist used to obtain his highlights. We can even see exactly how the line of the lip has been touched up. It is the work of a master-colourist using light to model his outlines, dabbing it on like powder; 'making up' the face of his model, as it were. Observe the skilful use made of the slight inflammation of the model's eye, which is repeated in the red of the lips and contrasted with the blue tone of the sclera, transforming an otherwise ash-grey picture into a work of vibrant colour contrast.

This close-up owes nothing to the careful analysis which painters were wont to devote to the texture of the model's skin. It is first and foremost an artistic triumph and only incidentally a portrait. If we compare it with the work of the contemporaneous artist Corneille de Lyon, its full originality becomes apparent. Only in the works of Antoine Caron and in the experiments of the Fontainebleau school does French painting show comparable freedom of treatment. With them, it was a question of giving free rein to their fancy, and their works had none of the austerity of this painting with its highly original simplification of volumes. The harmonious realism, the obvious truth of this portrait heralds the artistic revolution of the succeeding century by which court ceremonial was to be replaced by realistic everyday scenes.

152

LOUIS LE NAIN (1598–1648)   c. 1640
VISITING GRANDMOTHER   Oil on canvas
Catalogue No. 1172   Height 58 cm. (22³/₄″)
                                                  Width 73 cm. (28³/₄″)

It is tempting to consider the Le Nain brothers as no more than minor masters. After all, they produced only a few small, dull-toned pictures, one very like another and unspectacular beside the works of contemporaries such as Velasquez, Rembrandt, Caravaggio or Rubens. None of the brothers became one of those official painters whose talents received full licence from society. In none of them can we discover the evolution of a man's ideas, his struggle with his times, his heaven and his hell. Measured by such standards, clearly the Le Nain brothers do not 'make the grade'. And yet, in a gallery overflowing with seventeenth-century portraits of peasants, drinkers and musicians, painted with an immense display of ingenuity in composition, in interplay of light and shade, and in contrasting colours, it is often just the Le Nain pictures that seem to offer something different. Why is it that their unpretentious scenes, their stolid figures move us more than all the skilful animation, the clever virtuosity of others? Why, once noticed, are their pictures not forgotten, in spite of the less obvious nature of their charm? The answer is completely down-to-earth. Quite simply – genius. But genius under iron control; genius of that exacting kind which deliberately chooses its most banal form of expression.

The alignment of the figures, the placing of the faces side by side is here, of course, deliberate. Louis Le Nain could perfectly well have justified their presence by the usual groupings of figures ostensibly engaged in some plausible activity. Yet, contrary to both rule and custom, they stand surprisingly in line. In addition, two open doors shed light on both sides and give the nine figures (a tenth stands on the threshold as if expressly to mitigate the brilliance of the sky which stretches away to the horizon) the appearance of an array of heroes in one of those sparse but imposing settings now in vogue. The décor has a classical air: a moulded chimney looking rather like a pillar, a series of vertical lines cut by the triangle of light which illuminates the upper half of the old woman and drops to the feet of the smallest figure on the right. Note, too, how Le Nain animates the painting, in spite of the strict alignment, by placing each figure either a little in front of or just behind its neighbour. The young woman is thus almost effaced by the shadow of the child she carries, yet there is no insistence on the curious contours traced by the play of light on face and clothes. The way he grades his colours – from pink to rose through a series

154

of whites and greys back to red—also contributes to the rhythm of the picture. Such a work bears little relation to its title and refuses to be tied down to its size. We can scarcely say whether it is large or small. We are captivated to the point where dimensions are forgotten and only those created by the work itself are of importance—a sure sign of a complete artistic triumph.

Formerly Crozat Collection.

LOUIS LE NAIN (1598–1648) c. 1640
THE MILKMAID'S FAMILY Oil on canvas
Catalogue No. 1152 Height 51 cm. (20″)
Width 59 cm. (23¼″)

If this same subject had been treated by a Dutchman, he would, no doubt, have picked a country setting, complete with cows, or else some village farmyard. There would certainly have been some action: some attempt to tell a story. Here we have only silence. Le Nain has set his peasant family on a hilltop, expressly so that they may stand alone against the sky, their proportions thus appearing truly monumental, and has taken care to see that they are not mere silhouettes but completely solid figures. He has deliberately attempted a challenging composition ranged, as it were, against space; to offset the man in the broad-brimmed hat, he has used only the brightest of blues, an azure tongue between the clouds, dipping down towards the horizon, just as all the rest – the stick across the barrels, the position of the boy – also slant down towards the distant landscape, whose delicacy contrasts strongly with the minute detail of the donkey's coat, the costumes and the faces.

Whereas another painter might have shown the rich crops, the abundant pasturage, Le Nain's peasants have an almost abstract relationship with the land: more man and fatherland than cowherd and clover-crop. Should this seem too 'recherché' it must not be forgotten that, obsessed by our memories of Van Ostade and Steen, and always on the look-out for the rustic charm then flourishing in Europe, we tend to think of Le Nain always in his village, and among his peasants. Le Nain, however, was something more than this: he was the pioneer of a difficult intellectual experiment, exemplified elsewhere only in the work of Vermeer and Cézanne. Vermeer has also been regarded as just one more Dutch interior painter among many, and Cézanne's isolation in his southern countryside, far from the Parisian mêlée, has recently led to his being called 'primary' in comparison to Zola. Yet the truth lies elsewhere, in a subtle, solitary search for a quality which is perhaps only to be found far from the madding crowd.

It would, of course, be equally ridiculous to dissociate Le Nain from his subjects or to label him an abstract artist, painting peasants only because they were the fashionable models of his day. On the contrary, he painted them for his own pleasure; and these rough, ragged, ill-clad characters became the object of a highly original aesthetic venture, marked by a rejection of current artistic formulas and by a note of noble sobriety rarely found in art. Like Zurbaran, though more natural and more free and varied

in his treatment of the world of his invention, Le Nain was artistically an ascetic as subtle as he is impenetrable. Probably his painting, like Cézanne's did not come easily, each detail being battled over, each decision the outcome of a long, intense struggle. To mention just one example of his constant forethought: while the feet of all the figures in this picture remain (with one exception) invisible, although they stand full-height upon an eminence, we may be sure that this is not due to any negligence but to a deliberate desire to create a homogeneous unit, sculptural in form, centred on the figure of the donkey.

157

NICOLAS POUSSIN (1594–1665)　　　　　　　　　　　c. 1630
THE DEPOSITION　　　　　　　　　　　　　　　　　　Oil on canvas
Catalogue No. 1200　　　　　　　　　　　Height 119.5 cm. (47″)
　　　　　　　　　　　　　　　　　　　　　　Width 99 cm. (39″)

Poussin arrived in Rome in 1624. Although the first years were none too easy for him it was not long before he became known to connoisseurs, particularly after Cardinal Barberini commissioned him to paint a 'Death of Germanicus' and he had completed his huge 'Martyrdom of Erasmus' for St Peter's (1629). By 1630, the dealers had found their way to his studio in the Via del Babuino, where he had set up house with his newly-married young wife Anne-Marie Dughet. What were Poussin's interests at this time? He was working on the nude in the studio of Dominiquin, studying Raphael and Jules Romain, copying classical models and even going so far as to try his hand at modelling. At the same time he was reading the art treatises of Dürer and Alberti, in an attempt to learn all the secrets of optics and geometry. His work was thus based on careful and methodical preparation. His originality, however, did not immediately become apparent, manifesting itself only at a later date, in the 'Bacchanalia', in the great landscapes, and in compositions such as 'The Inspiration of the Poet' and 'Arcadian Shepherds'. Poussin was seeking here, not to express a personal note but to solve the problems presented by a certain subject, or a certain composition. For him, art was primarily a science, that of 'imitating in line and colour everything under the sun'. This is his own definition, but probably he did not observe the letter of its law, for it is not so much a programme as a declaration of a universal freedom which Poussin was far from claiming for himself. His figures are clothed in the conventional garments of 'noble' art, his cities are archaeological reconstructions. Yet, within this rigid framework, this strict discipline, these purely classical terms, he contrived to convey something never before expressed. Perhaps this was because he came to classicism at a time when it represented not the academic but the avant-garde.

This 'Deposition' occupies a unique place in his work. It certainly owes its inspiration to the great Venetians, for whom he expressed an obstinate and very non-conformist admiration when in Rome. But Venetian though it is, both in lighting and in colour, the painting is still strongly characteristic of Poussin. His originality can clearly be seen in the treatment of the draperies and the painting of the angels.

Formerly Bruhl Collection.

NICOLAS POUSSIN (1594–1665)　　　　　　　　　c. 1630
Tancred and Erminia　　　　　　　　　　　Oil on canvas
Catalogue No. 1189　　　　　　　　　　　Height 98.5 cm. (38¹/₈")
　　　　　　　　　　　　　　　　　　Width 146.5 cm. (57³/₄")

This picture (a masterpiece in modern eyes) was followed some few years
later by another version loaded with antiquarian detail and fluttering
cupids. For Poussin considered each of his pictures as an individual exercise
in a given style to be executed to the very best of his ability. Here sobriety
is the keynote. In the other (Birmingham) version, the rhythm is much livelier, but both versions are valid contributions to the theme. The broad horizontal lines and the bareness of the earth impart to the Hermitage picture a
dreamlike stillness. The rents in Erminia's tunic, the calm of the wounded
Tancred, the long rhythmic curves of the central group and of the horse to
the left of the picture, have almost a musical quality. At the same time, the
snow-white horse, resembling some creature from another world, seems to
transport us into the realms of near-fantasy.

NICOLAS POUSSIN (1594–1665) 1657
THE REST ON THE FLIGHT INTO EGYPT Oil on canvas
Catalogue No. 6741 Height 105 cm. (41¼")
 Width 145 cm. (57¼")

Poussin maintained that Caravaggio's was a highly dangerous example and
that his sole achievement had been to destroy painting. We can easily see
why this calm and classical landscape artist should have failed to appreciate
a portrait painter with a penchant for bad characters, a painter of equivocal
shadows. Poussin's approach to the classical admitted no hint of mockery.
The merit of this picture lies not only in its rendering of the mellow quiet of
a summer evening, but also in the light it throws on Poussin's interest in
antiquity: the artist first carefully studied the mosaic discovered by Cardinal Barberini underneath his palace, depicting a procession of the priests
of Sarapis, with their greyhound statues and the sacred ibis on the towers.
 Formerly Stroganov Collection.

CLAUDE LORRAIN (1600–1682)   c. 1649
MORNING (EVENING) AT THE PORT   Oil on canvas
Catalogue No. 1243   Height 97.5 cm. (38¹/₄″)
                                                         Width 120.5 cm. (47¹/₄″)

This picture has several different titles. Somov calls it 'Evening at a port':
Charles Sterling also sees in it a sunset, whereas in the latest catalogue of the
Hermitage it figures as 'Morning at a port'. Probably it is on account of the
chests on which the figures are seated and the young woman's beckoning
gesture that the editors have opted for a departure and therefore for a sun-
rise. On the other hand, one of the men seems to have begun to discharge
the dinghy which nears the shore, suggesting landfall at eventide. In the last
resort it matters little, however, since the picture is equally moving either
way, for it shows that the artist was seeking to do more than merely describe
a specific maritime activity. Looking at it, we experience a number of emotions: exaltation on the threshold of the infinite; the heightened tension of
the moment when earth and sky merge in a single blaze of golden dust; and,
finally, a faint feeling of amazement at the classical Triumphal Arch which
still stands, crumbling but yielding not, ready to endure for centuries to
come though it has become obsolete in a port which great ships no longer
enter. Why did Claude Lorrain paint so many ports like this one and what
did his admirers see in them? A shared dream, perhaps, in which the Lor-
rainer indulges in his longing for the south, for heat, for sun, for spreading
pines, warm seas and classical antiquity.

    Claude Lorrain used to rise before dawn to paint the actual scene, going
out again at evening to catch the setting sun and watch day descend into
night. As Goethe said, 'His pictures are at once completely true and totally
devoid of all reality.' The sole reality sought by Lorrain in the woods and
on the beaches was that of light: the rest was his invention – the gradual
discovery from one painting to another of his own particular paradise,
composed of elements selected according to the dictates of fantasy, or, more
strictly, of his heart.

    In the Europe of his day a landscape was perforce a composition. The
artist did not restrict himself to the village or the fields which lay before
his eyes. In depicting nature he endeavoured to evoke the whole world,
its rhythm and its meaning. The merest tree recalled the miracle of creation.
Lorrain's contribution was of cardinal importance in this respect, for it was
he who deprived the landscape of these edifying elements, introducing an
altogether different scale of values – those of man's relation to his inner
dream. To accomplish this required the simple courage of a simple man.

History tells us that in artistic Roman circles Lorrain never passed for a clever painter, a connoisseur of classical proportion. When Poussin, in his turn, took to painting landscapes, he treated them as the closest possible reconstruction of reality, without a single element of fantasy in portraiture of tree or stone. Linden and sandstone must be immediately identifiable. Into this tamed, easily recognizable, well-labelled world, it was possible to fit several lovely legends. Even in his most deeply felt works Poussin remains always his own master. Claude Lorrain, however, is completely unconstrained: confident in his own sensitivity, and in his dreams; basically, an Impressionist.

Originally in the Sir Robert Walpole Collection.

ANTOINE WATTEAU (1684–1721)   c. 1709
THE SAVOYARD   Oil on canvas
Catalogue No. 1148   Height 40.5 cm. (16")
                                                          Width 32.5 cm. (12¹/₂")

Watteau's work is always difficult to date. This young Savoyard with his marmot, set against a landscape more reminiscent of the Ile de France than of the north, is certainly an early work; we are inclined to date it before the composition called: 'What have I done? Accursed assassins!' – an anti-medical *scène de théâtre* treated in the Hermitage catalogue as Watteau's earliest work though the handling is considerably more free than in the case of our Savoyard. But experts place this picture at the time of Watteau's return to Valenciennes. At the beginning of the century the artist, it will be remembered, had left for Paris, where he lived from hand to mouth, working first in the studio of Claude Gillot and later in that of Charles Audran, prior to competing for the Grand Prix de Rome. The subject set was 'David's return after the defeat of Goliath', and the winner was not Watteau but a docile student by the name of Antoine Grison, of whom nothing more was ever heard. After this failure Watteau returned to Valenciennes, where, at the age of 25, he is said to have produced this picture. It remains a unique experiment on his part. While memories of Dutch peasant scenes may account for some features (Watteau is said at one point to have earned his bread by copying the works of Van Ostade), the main inspiration is rather that of Louis Le Nain, tempered by a new touch of malice. Le Nain springs to mind because the picture is no improvised scene à la Van Ostade but shows a full-length figure motionless against the background.

The treatment of the Savoyard is somewhat laboured. The background, on the other hand, deserves our full attention, for it is the only modern landscape in the whole of Watteau's work. In later years, the artist drew only a 'noble' architecture, composed of distant temples and backdrop palaces.

Here, the leafless trees seem to be a-quiver with a feathery incandescence, anticipating Sisley. The houses are the houses that Sisley and Monet later painted, for the French landscape changes little. And finally, the landscape is set like a frieze between the blue sky, its clouds billowing above the housetops and church steeple, and the earth, alive with strokes designed rather to break the flatness of the colour than to represent actual blades of grass. Is this, then, a composition whose austerity is deliberate, or simply one of Watteau's earliest experiments in painting?

Formerly Audran Collection.

164

ANTOINE WATTEAU (1684–1721)   c. 1712 or 1717
CHARACTERS FROM THE *Commedia dell'Arte*   Oil on wood
Catalogue No. 1131   Height 20 cm. (7⁷/₈″)
                                           Width 25 cm. (9⁷/₈″)

This work is not far removed from the close-packed pages of the sketch-books which Watteau filled with countless heads, drawn from life or invented. It has been called indiscriminately 'The return from the Ball' and 'Departure for the Ball' and 'The coquette'. It can also be taken to be a series of different characters from the *Commedia dell'Arte:* the ingénue, the masked countess, the old peasant, and the negro, rather a crowded scene to find within the frame of such a tiny picture. Watteau, like Le Nain, was fond of such alignments, offering as they did an opportunity for contrasting faces. Perhaps such pictures answer best to the name of studies. Closely constructed as any Clouet, they display the virtuosity of a palette ranging from dull blue to purple, in which the bronzed face of the young man, the fresh Rubens-like features of the ingénue and the round black ball of the negro's head are contrasted. And then, for good measure, the rustling lace on cap and collar. Furs, woollens, cottons, silks – all the materials are so admirably differentiated that a dress designer would probably have little difficulty in identifying them today. This picture is as concise as any miniature, brimming with truth and accurate observation, well able to stand enlargment to life-size. Watteau's art has been described as no more than an aura of charm. He was, however, also capable of the careful realism of this painting; nor should we forget that behind each figure of his 'Fêtes Galantes' were dozens of acutely observed sketches in which the pencil seems almost literally to dissect the model, though no trace of all this appears in the final picture.

Here is one of Watteau's buyers speaking of his client's work: 'This artist makes pictures in much the same way that Monsieur Lesage makes books and comedies. The only difference is that whereas Lesage is sometimes satisfied with his books and with his comedies, poor Watteau is never satisfied with his pictures. He has promised me a "Fair at Lendit", which will be a masterpiece if he ever manages to put the finishing touches to it. If, however, one of his black moods comes over him, he'll go off at a tangent and it's good-bye to the masterpiece.' Watteau was by this time a sick man: tuberculosis left him only ten years to live after his return to Paris – ten years in which to accomplish all his work, a total of 217 pictures.

Formerly Crozat Collection.

166

ANTOINE WATTEAU (1684–1721)   c. 1718
CAPRICE   Oil on canvas
Catalogue No. 4120   Height 42 cm. (16½")
             Width 34 cm. (13½")

Open skies, a park and a gown of black satin. A hand crumpling the light among satin folds, to create a myriad glinting rivulets. Beyond that, only the roughly sketched silhouette of a man, an expanse of grass, some barely budding trees and a few vague figures in the distance. The scene might equally well be Versailles or some corner of Watteau's own imaginary world, an evanescent world of china figurines and marionettes dressed in all their finery, playing their parts in some mysterious comedy. Later, Watteau came to compose paintings of much deeper meaning, of figures resplendent in bosky glades. Here, however, we have just the opposite: an open sky, almost barren ground, and, in the centre, two costumed figures set against a delicate screen of trees. Watteau is known to have been a devotee of Rubens, from whom he learned his vivid brushwork, and perhaps the freshness of his quickly sketched-in faces. Watteau, however, rejected both the lyricism and the decorative style of Rubens. 'Seize eloquence and wring its neck' – Watteau would have agreed with Verlaine on this as on other issues. He was all for simplicity and unselfconsciousness: no gestures, no grandiloquence, but a deliberate sobriety.

Watteau was by this time a member of the Royal Academy beside such men as Rigaud, Largillière, Le Clerc and Desportes. What can these artists have thought of his vital, vivid art, painted with the lightest of brushes, sometimes almost hasty in appearance? Admiration would have required foreknowledge of the fact that Watteau's brief career contained in essence the charm of the whole coming century. Nattier, Oudry, Lancret, Pater were his juniors. Boucher was nineteen years younger, Greuze was born four, Fragonard almost fifty years after his death. Watteau's artistic progeny were to flourish for many a year, but when at last the lights of his Fête Champêtre were dimmed, he suffered a long eclipse. His painting was, however, in an age-old tradition. Happy figures under open skies are also found in the paintings of the 'hortus deliciarum' artists of the Middle Ages, in the paradises depicted by sixteenth-century painters, in the gardens where, in the following century, Susanna bathed before the Elders, as well as in the mechanical mazes of the eighteenth-century. For has not 'Garden' always been a synonym for 'Paradise'?

Formerly Stroganov Collection.

168

ANTOINE WATTEAU (1684–1721)
THE EMBARRASSING PROPOSAL
Catalogue No. 1150

c. 1711
Oil on canvas
Height 65 cm. (25¹/₂″)
Width 84.5 cm. (33¹/₄″)

What are these elegant creatures doing in the forest glade? Probably per-
forming some play, singing to a guitar accompaniment, or trying out the
steps of a new dance. Watteau deliberately painted his figures almost in
silhouette. Their backs are turned, partly to display their costumes, and
partly to tone down yet further a picture in which everything, even the
sound of the half-concealed guitar, was already muted. Watteau, like Claude
Lorrain, was a poet of light, pursuing from picture to picture his somewhat
melancholy vision of rich and exquisite textures.

Formerly Bruhl Collection.

NICOLAS LANCRET (1690–1743)   c. 1730
THE DANCER, LA CAMARGO
Catalogue No. 1145   Height 45 cm. (17³/₄″)
                         Width 55 cm. (21³/₄″)

No one should look at a Lancret after looking at a Watteau. The master's smile becomes the pupil's simper, and Watteau's ethereal figures decline into clumsy figurines. Lancret should never have repeated Watteau's themes, and the success of the younger man, on whom he had so often urged the virtues of originality, understandably annoyed Watteau. Lancret enjoyed early a fame which came to Watteau only late in life. Round about 1730 he painted several canvases (Wallace Collection, Nantes and Potsdam Museum) of the twenty-year-old La Camargo dancing in her open-air theatre.

JEAN-BAPTISTE SIMEON CHARDIN (1699–1779)   1766

THE ATTRIBUTES OF THE ARTS   Oil on canvas

Catalogue No. 5627   Height 112 cm. (43¹/₄″)

Width 140.5 cm. (55¹/₈″)

Chardin's work is in the great Dutch tradition of still-life and interior painting. Yet when this son of a Parisian cabinet-maker from St Germain-des-Prés, newly graduated from the workshops of Cazes and Coypel, was ready to execute his first orders, he was called to Fontainebleau to restore the frescoes of Rosso and Primatice. Aesthetically speaking, the experiment was a failure. Large-scale decorative painting held no appeal for Chardin. The first picture he ever exhibited – in the open-air salon in the Place Dauphine – was a still-life, and to this type of painting he remained faithful all his life, painting figures only in his smaller canvases. To contemporary artists such as Latour, Lancret, Nattier, he owes nothing. Holland was his constant source of inspiration: when his painting is least good, it resembles that of Ter Borch. But most of his scenes show great originality, conveying, oddly enough for the unfortunate father of a son who died by his own hand, delightful evocations of the world of childhood. Nevertheless, works like 'Child with Teetotum' or 'Benedicite' remain for him mere light flights of fancy. His epic struggles were always with still-life subjects – for him this was the heroic genre – in which he achieved real grandeur.

Chardin deliberately chose not to join the ranks of those who painted princely silverware and priceless porcelains. Perhaps we need not even look as far afield as Holland for the origin of his earthen pots, his wicker baskets and his copper bowls. For these he could have had no better master than Louis le Nain, to whom he turned for inspiration in the best of his interiors. Chardin leaned naturally towards the simple, finding excitement in revealing the beauty of a common object, often previously unperceived even by its owner. Although his works are not all dated, they appear to evolve in the direction of ever-increasing simplicity. At first he sets the scene upon his table cloth, slicing a sausage, perhaps, or upsetting a glass. But he was quick to realize the futility of such incidentals and his greatest still-lifes depend only on the brilliance of the light as it falls upon some everyday object like a jug. His colour too is as if drenched with light; it has a soft, almost creamy quality. His tones are juxtaposed, without the usual transitions, revealing skilfully controlled power; the artist dims or heightens them according to the demands of each particular composition. Thus his work has a singular velvety quality. Composed of a number of symbolic objects (the traditional tools of the painter and the architect, together with Pigalle's

'Mercury' to symbolize sculpture), this still-life suggests not disorder and abundance but order and moderation. Designed for Catherine II to decorate the top of a doorway, it is a work which, though intended purely as a modest ornament, can stand up to prolonged analysis.

FRANÇOIS BOUCHER (1703–1770)
HEAD OF A WOMAN
Catalogue No. 5635

Oil on canvas
Height 36 cm. (14¹/₄")
Width 28 cm. (11")

According to the Goncourt brothers, Boucher's work 'sums up the taste of his whole century, constituting an expression, a personification, an incarnation even of that taste.' Although he was far from being the most original artist of his time, the century of Louis XV would certainly not have been the same without him. Without Boucher, Olympus would not have fallen prey to gallantry, Diana would not have assumed the features of a marquise, and the ladies of the court would never have had the exquisite pleasure of finding themselves surprised at their toilet by an artist in the role of Actaeon. Boucher was indeed so well matched to his era that it ended by dominating him.

Admittedly, he seems to have yielded to the temptation to paint pot-boilers, since his earliest known works are pious images, clearly the standard holy pictures of the day. Although Watteau also began his career in the back room of a dealer in mass-produced Dutch interiors, in his case no one noted these commercial chores or drew attention to them. Boucher was, however, to pay a heavy price for so much facility – at the height of his success, having become a painter-of-all-work for the society of his day, he overdid the production of his 'scènes galantes'. A sudden change of taste followed, and Diderot, who had formerly sung his praises, wrote that 'Boucher is only good for turning the heads of society figures and of artists. His elegance, his grace, one might even say his depravity, have no charm for any but minor masters. Artists who can recognize his technical skill – and praise it all the more because only they can appreciate it fully – bow down before him, making him their god. But to men of discrimination, who prefer the discipline of the classical, he is of no account whatever.'

The most charming and least serious painter of all time was doomed to disappear under an avalanche of Roman ruins and heroes of antiquity. Yet his detractors might well have recognized, for example in this sober 'Head of a Woman', evidence of his indisputable talent. Boucher's favourite feminine type has been here endowed with an unusual reflective note of tenderness, and we cannot but admire the bold line, the gentle illumination of the forms, the incandescence of the flesh itself. 'His name will scarcely be remembered,' continued Diderot remorselessly. Yet, looking at this picture, we recognize the bold hand of a master.

Formerly Youssupoff Collection.

JEAN-HONORE FRAGONARD (1732–1806)

THE STOLEN KISS
Catalogue No. 1300

Oil on canvas
Height 46 cm. (18¹/₈″)
Width 55 cm. (21⁵/₈″)

Charles Natoire, Director of the Academy of Rome was visited by Fragonard, as by each successive winner of the Prix de Rome, and described his caller in the following terms: 'Considerable talent, but his excitable, impatient temperament prevents him from devoting himself carefully enough to his copying.' Admittedly, before he left for Rome, Fragonard had been warned by Boucher not to pay over-much attention to the Michelangelo's and Raphaels. 'Take them all seriously and you will be done for,' said the master. And so the obedient pupil preferred to admire such painters as were doubtless more in keeping with his own gay and light-hearted nature: Barocci, Solimena and Tiepolo. Moreover, the important thing is not so much what he admired (his enthusiams led him to produce a delirious composition entitled 'Coresus and Callirhoë' which gained him entry into the Academy) but what he saw and what he drew: an Italian countryside no longer pompous and ennobled, but springing naturally and with renewed vigour from his pencil. In his pictures all is fleeting, fluttering, centred on some billowing cloud or ethereal bustle.

In comparison with the tangled curlicues of certain better-known works, however, the picture reproduced here seems relatively calm. This will perhaps make it easier for those disconcerted by his usual breathless rhythms to appreciate the talent displayed in this tranquil scene. The composition has been determined by the incident recorded. A young woman seeking her scarf has left the salon where her friends are still at cards. Enter a young gallant who draws her to him and in whose embrace she fears to be discovered. The picture can also be assessed from a different standpoint: a diagonal line of light cuts across the composition between the two perpendiculars of the open doors. There are fine contrasting rhythms in the hooped skirt, the pattern on the carpet, the chair back and the round frame barely discernible in the background. The light caresses the throat of the young woman, the brilliance of her dress and her silken scarf, whose transparency is most skilfully conveyed.

The dress and scarf put us in mind of Watteau. Yet Watteau appears almost a primitive in comparison with Fragonard, who, in his outdoor scenes, remains the last and greatest baroque painter of the eighteenth century.

Originally in the Collection of King Stanislaus Augustus of Poland.

176

EUGENE DELACROIX (1798–1863) 1855
MOROCCAN SADDLING HIS HORSE Oil on canvas
Catalogue No. 3852 Height 56 cm. (22″)
Width 47 cm. (18¹/₂″)

After his conquest of Algeria, Louis Philippe of France was anxious to reach friendly terms with his powerful neighbour the Sultan of Morocco. For this reason he decided in 1832 to dispatch an embassy to Morocco to which was attached, as artistic recorder of the mission, the painter Delacroix, then aged 34. Ever since the exhibition of his 'Dante and Virgil' ten years previously, he had been famous, subsequent paintings having included the 'Massacre of Chios', the 'Death of Sardanapalus' and 'Liberty leading the People'. He was the most brilliant of the younger generation and this journey to Morocco and Algeria was to mark a vital step in his career. After six months, Delacroix returned with those thousands of drawings and water colours which were to serve as a source of inspiration throughout his life. This brief stay was enough to make him an orientalist for life. The Orient he sought in Morocco was in fact antiquity in terms of the living: men not monuments. 'Imagine what it is like', runs a letter to a friend, 'to see lying in the sun, walking in the streets, or mending shoes by the roadside the figure of a Roman Consul, a Cato or a Brutus.' He was struck by the originality of costumes and customs and by the grandeur of nature, fully expecting to see lions in the desert and taking great pleasure, even thirty years after his journey, in making a second painting of the Sultan Abder Rahman and his guard. His romanticism, if indeed it was romanticism, joined forces with classical antiquity on the slopes of the Atlas Mountains.

This 'Moroccan saddling his horse', painted twenty-three years after his Moroccan visit, from drawings carefully preserved in his sketchbook, is Venetian in its colouring. But the horse is an Arab charger, and the actual brushwork is of yet another time and race. His method of conveying shape by the use of colour is more sharply marked than ever and a new freedom is discernible in his treatment of the horse's neck. Delacroix never handled colour more powerfully than in this picture, where it assumes the quality of enamel.

Formerly Kuchelev Collection and Musée des Beaux Arts, Paris.

CAMILLE COROT (1796–1875)   c. 1860
RECOLLECTIONS OF PIERREFONDS   Oil on canvas
                                                 Height 46 cm. (18″)
                                                 Width 38 cm. (15″)

Claude Lorrain's contemporaries insisted that he was no painter. Likewise, when Corot was approaching fifty, his father was heard to say: 'Camille? Oh, yes, a charming boy, but most unlikely ever to get anywhere with his painting.' It is true that while battles raged in the Salon over contemporary painting, Corot's works were never called in question. He was, in fact, as badly neglected by his contemporaries as had been Claude Lorrain, his acknowledged master, before him.

What made his contemporaries so blind? Was it because he was exclusively a landscape artist; that is, one who was content with a minor genre during a period when historical painting was still carrying all before it? Was it because the subtlety of his vision was lost among so many more pretentious compositions? Today, Corot ranks far higher than any of those who triumphed in the days of his eclipse.

Never a conscious revolutionary, Corot remained outwardly extremely close to Poussin and to Lorrain. In his pictures we find sweeping landscapes where Homer still plays his lyre to listening shepherds, Diana still takes her bath, and naked women are still labelled Nymphs and Bacchantes. Such conventionality conveyed a false impression. The world did not recognize how audacious were his figures of featureless women, ignored the powerful landscapes created from the reflection of a patch of blue sky in a pond, or from some wayside church. Corot quietly applied his poetic brush to all those landscapes before which the Impressionists were in course of time to set their easels.

The castle of Pierrefonds was a fourteenth-century masterpiece, transformed into a second masterpiece by Viollet-le-Duc. With Corot it was so favoured a subject that between 1840 and 1845 he painted several different pictures, one of which he modified in 1867, the castle having been restored in 1862. Between 1850 and 1860 the painter himself restored, in his imagination, the great fortress, depicting it as it had been in the days of its glory. He merely suggests a silhouette in the faint light of early dawn, hinting in the foreground at two soldiers with glinting lance and helmet. These and the distant towers suggest that the bourgeois Corot was not insensitive to romantic themes, though he did not allow them to disturb his tranquil vision.

At present in the Pushkin Museum, Moscow.

CLAUDE MONET (1840–1926)   c. 1867
WOMAN IN A GARDEN   Oil on canvas
Catalogue No. 6505   Height 80 cm. (31$^{1}/_{2}$")
            Width 99 cm. (39")

This early work of Monet's was painted at Sainte-Adresse, near Le Havre, in the garden of his aunt Lecadre, with whom he had sought refuge from his penury. This was a particularly unhappy period in the artist's life, for his aunt had agreed to take him in only on condition that he should separate from the young woman then expecting his child. The summer over, Monet rejoined Camille and his son, deliberately choosing a life of poverty.

The whole of Impressionism is already contained in this picture.

Formerly Schukin Collection.

CLAUDE MONET (1840–1926) c. 1886
FIELD OF POPPIES Oil on canvas
Catalogue No. 9004 Height 59 cm. (23¹/₄″)
Width 90 cm. (35¹/₂″)

In what essential does this landscape differ from those painted by Diaz or Corot? Surely, the fact that what we appreciate in this summer scene is more the style of painting than the subject itself.

The Impressionist battle has now been won and Monet no longer needs to drive himself so hard. He will not set up his easel unless the site provides him with the necessary compulsion. From certain villages he flees in haste, unable to find anything to paint. Elsewhere he will be seized with a bout of enthusiasm, painting unremittingly, often conscious of falling short of the truth. Thus Monet, the master acclaimed today by the most abstract of colourists, may well have considered himself to be a realist.

Formerly Morosov Collection.

AUGUSTE RENOIR (1841–1919)   1877
PORTRAIT OF JEANNE SAMARY   Oil on canvas
Height 56 cm. (22″)
Width 47 cm. (18½″)

A frank, slightly upturned face; dominating it, a pair of compelling eyes, their colour changing with the changing light, that was Jeanne Samary. From the moment he first made her acquaintance at the house of the publisher Charpentier, Renoir was an enthusiastic admirer of this young actress from the Comédie Française. She died young, and had we not Renoir's portraits, she would now be little more than a name. 'A delightful girl with a wonderful skin,' commented Renoir. 'She actually seems to shed light around her.' The painter had only to set this charming source of light against a series of backgrounds varying from green to pink, enhancing her delicate features by the addition of green shadows which made her appear even blonder than in actual life, and Jeanne Samary was transformed into 'a Renoir'.

Setting aside the somewhat laboured full-length portrait also in the Hermitage, which of the two other Samary portraits – that in the Hermitage or that in the Comédie Française – is the better? The picture reproduced opposite is certainly the more audacious. Only the eyes, mouth and eyebrows, together with a few strands of hair have been drawn in. Not a single other feature is apparent. A kind of coloured radiance seems to blur the outlines of neck, shoulders and arms. It is as if a haze of colour emanated from the forms themselves. Renoir was right: Jeanne Samary's flesh did indeed shed light. The pearly whiteness of her skin communicates itself to the pink background in a radiance rarely attained even by Renoir. Later he tried to achieve radiance by other means than the use of a single colour. His colour here is brilliant and triumphant: the free brushstrokes vibrate, and it is as though a myriad sunbeams were dancing across the canvas. The painter has thrown logic to the winds and intensifies or dims his values purely for the visual pleasure thus obtained and for the clearer expression of his joy. It has been said, on the one hand that this is Renoir's most Impressionist portrait, and on the other that it is the one which tells us most about his model. The two qualities are not necessarily incompatible. In contrast to the somewhat vacant look of some of Renoir's models, the eyes of Jeanne Samary look us straight in the face as if wishing to convince us of the joy of life.

Formerly Morosov Collection; at present in the Pushkin Museum, Moscow.

184

AUGUSTE RENOIR (1841–1919)   1881
Two Girls in Black   Oil on canvas
                                                  Height 80 cm. (31¹/₂")
                                                   Width 65 cm. (25¹/₂")

One day in the forest of Fontainebleau a great lumbering figure limped up
to the young Renoir and said, 'It's not bad. But why do you use so much
black?' It was Narcisse Diaz who thus encouraged on the road to artistic
freedom the twenty-two-year-old Renoir, still heavily encumbered with
the principles inculcated by Gleyre and the pundits of the Ecole des Beaux-
Arts. But the way to artistic freedom was long, and Renoir reached the
age of twenty-six before, abandoning accurate drawing, 'leché' and 'rendu',
he ventured to show the blue tinge of a white dress in shadow. Nothing
was basically altered by this experiment; on the contrary, it contributed
to the natural evolution of his genius, so that the nudes of his maturity
bear a strong resemblance to his youthful work 'Diana, the huntress'.

All this to introduce the blackness which Diaz claimed to be holding up
Renoir's evolution. In this painting his black is no longer mere shadow – the
classical means of denoting space – but a brilliant colour in its own right.

Formerly Schukin Collection; at present in the Pushkin Museum, Moscow.

AUGUSTE RENOIR (1841–1919)   c. 1881–2
WOMAN WITH A FAN   Oil on canvas
Catalogue No. 6507   Height 65 cm. (25¹/₂″)
                                              Width 50 cm. (19³/₄″)

A typical Renoir portrait of an unknown model. This artist is alleged to
have painted many of his figures without models. Certainly he was technically capable of so doing, though it seems improbable that he would have
voluntarily deprived himself of the pleasure of looking at a pretty girl
while he worked. However this may be, he certainly took from his models
only what suited his taste and they have therefore all a certain family
resemblance. His figures are – to use terminology of abstract art – pro-
jections of his own personality; they disregard the rules and are unaffected
by extraneous considerations. All his life Renoir painted the same woman:
his technique alone evolved. While Monet sought in nature the inspiration
necessary to his artistic creation, painting over and over again the same
landscape, Renoir, for his part, concentrated upon the female form: his
painting was first and foremost an expression of love.

Historians have made much of Renoir's somewhat distant attitude to
Impressionism as personified by its orthodox leader Claude Monet, quoting
as proof of their estrangement Renoir's famous 'Ingres' period. These,
however, are mere details, for the artistic theories of Impressionism are
far less important than the freedom it conferred upon the artist.

This figure with a fan constitutes one of Renoir's boldest experiments.
'In the early days,' he said, 'I used to lay on my greens and yellows in
layers thinking that this increased their value. Then one day it struck
me that Rubens achieved more by a mere touch than I with all my layers.'
Look at this picture: the paint is applied with a lightness of touch that
seems almost as casual as that of Matisse; it is as if all the colour had
been absorbed, leaving only a fine powder. Certainly the outlines are firmer
than in the portrait of Jeanne Samary, but we are still far from the
precision of the Ingres period. The clarity of this picture springs from the
contrast of light and dark, and Renoir has achieved a tour de force by
preserving against so pale and luminous a background the integrity of
the surface of the white fan, reflecting a whole range of colours, an over-all
pictorial unity undisturbed even by the darker patches of the hair and
jabot. Renoir's art was subtle in the extreme, a matter of pin-point
equilibrium.

Formerly Morosov Collection.

188

LIVERPOOL COLLEGE OF ART

AUGUSTE RENOIR (1841–1919)   1885
CHILD WITH A WHIP   Oil on canvas
Catalogue No. 9006   Height 105 cm. (41¼″)
                                    Width 75 cm. (29½″)

Renoir never painted elderly people. Even his self-portraits often appear half averted, as if the artist were escaping from himself. Renoir was never one for introspection: for him, beauty was outside a person. The private life of the man had nothing to do with the artist and, unlike Rembrandt and Van Gogh, only rarely did he seek to record something of his personality as reflected in the mirror. Probably the reason is that the skin of an adult man has not the same sheen as that of a woman or a child.

To appreciate this sheen to the full, Renoir liked to place his model in shadow, preferably in shadow cast by trees. The subject then seems to dispense a light of its own at least as bright as the sunbeams which pierce the vaulting trees and shimmer on the forest floor or garden grass.

Who was this child, armed with a whip, playing the role of dauntless coachman to a troop of excited cavaliers astride the donkeys in some Paris park? Renoir made little distinction between true portraits and mere figures: between works in which he was seeking a likeness, and the rest. And the reason why he seldom refused commissions for portraits was probably because they differed little from what he liked to paint when left to his own devices. He had no wish to capture movement, and when, on occasion, he painted a group of figures in profile, it was not so much for the sake of telling a story as to give additional importance to some carefully-posed central figure. We should not, however, forget that Renoir also painted a number of powerful rhythmic compositions, from the 'Moulin de la Galette' to the great nude groupings, by way of 'Les Canotiers' and 'Les Parapluies'. But these were the exceptions, specially intended for the Salon. As a rule Renoir's works are more direct, more immediate; what, in another age would no doubt have been labelled and exhibited as 'studies'.

This 'Child with a whip' dates from what is generally known as Renoir's 'Ingres' period, also sometimes referred to as his 'aigre' or 'sharp' period. How far this sharpness really went can be seen in this picture. The drawing is exact, the outlines clear, yet this precision does not in any way detract from the over-all radiance of the picture.

Formerly Morosov Collection.

EDGAR DEGAS (1834–1917)   1884
KNEELING WOMAN   Pastel
                               Height 50 cm. (19³/₄″)
                                Width 49 cm. (19¹/₂″)

The nudes of this type exhibited by Degas in 1886 caused a public scandal.
But Degas countered criticism by deploring the days when artists, knowing
nothing of 'women at the tub', painted only 'Susanna bathing'. Even though
the artist himself tells us that his intention was to show women as 'animals
in process of cleaning themselves', what strikes us most forcibly today is not so
much the naturalism of these works as the nobility of the art which they reveal.
    At present in the Puskin Museum, Moscow.

EDGAR DEGAS (1834 1917) c. 1885
WOMAN AT HER TOILET Pastel
Height 52 cm. (20¹/₄")
Width 51 cm. (20")

When in Italy at the age of twenty four, Degas often copied the compositions of Luca Signorelli, not as an academic exercise, but simply because in them he found something he was to love for as long as he lived – forms outlined like signs in space. Whether observing a dancer bending forward to adjust a slipper, or simply a woman washing her back, what he sought was a new form to be clothed in the richest possible colours.

At present in the Pushkin Museum, Moscow.

ALFRED SISLEY (1839–1899)   1884
BANKS OF THE SEINE AT SAINT-MAMMÈS   Oil on canvas
Catalogue No. 9167   Height 50 cm. (19³/₄″)
                                            Width 65 cm. (25¹/₂″)

Snow, sun or floodwater; all these were grist to Sisley's mill. Roads, canals, rivers, all were simply pathways beneath the greater pathway of the clouds. Not that Sisley dreamed of distant places, for he rarely left the Ile de France. Always a countryman at heart, Sisley was content to let his work remain a little outside the main current of the art of the big cities, although – as we see in this landscape, freer than the preceding one – he was by no means unaware of the evolution of Impressionism towards more vivid colouring. For him painting was more than a means of expression: it was above all a way of communing with nature. The countryside acted as an 'escape' for Sisley, the least fortunate of all the Impressionist painters.

   Formerly Morosov Collection.

ALFRED SISLEY (1839–1899)   1872
VILLAGE ON THE BANKS OF THE SEINE   Oil on canvas
Catalogue No. 9005   Height 59 cm. (23¹/₁″)
Width 80.5 cm. (33¹/₂″)

Although too much has been said of Monet's influence on Sisley, it would be absurd to deny it altogether. This landscape was painted in 1872, the same year in which Monet, trying out at Le Havre his 'Rising sun – an impression', revealed his liberation from the Corot school of landscapes constructed according to traditional architectural principles; the very principles to which Sisley remained faithful all his life. Alfred Sisley was the landscape artist par excellence. While the other Impressionists tackled almost every conceivable subject, the open air was his only studio.

Formerly Schukin Collection.

VINCENT VAN GOGH (1853–1890)   1888
THE SEA AT SAINTES-MARIES   Oil on Canvas
Height 44 cm. (17¹/₄″)
Width 53 cm. (20³/₄″)

'The sea has the changing colours of mackerel,' wrote Van Gogh from
Saintes-Maries to his brother Theo. In June 1888, he had moved from Arles
to the coast and the sight of the sea brought home to him the need
to 'exaggerate colour'. In fact, he found the Camargue 'exactly in Ruysdael's
style', with the result that this remarkably bold picture must be regarded
both as an avantgarde creation and as a classical Dutch seascape.

At present in the Pushkin Museum, Moscow.

196

VINCENT VAN GOGH (1853–1890)   1888
THE BUSH   Oil on canvas
Catalogue No. 6511   Height 73 cm. (28³/₄")
                                 Width 92 cm. (36¹/₄")

Van Gogh was enraptured by the flower-filled gardens and fields of
Provence – even the thistle-scattered patches of wasteland. 'I am working
at painting like a steam engine,' he wrote, and this unremitting work made
him more and more conscious of all that separated him from the Impressionists. 'What I learned in Paris is leaving me,' he told his brother.
The 'bush' of this picture marks a transition: still Impressionist, it testifies
to Van Gogh's individual ability to create flamboyant, moving works from
subjects generally considered the reverse of picturesque.

Formerly Schukin Collection.

VINCENT VAN GOGH (1853–1890) November 1888
THE AMPHITHEATRE, ARLES Oil on canvas
Catalogue No. 6529 Height 73 cm. (28³/₄″)
Width 92 cm. (36¹/₄″)

In 1888, Gauguin came to live with Vincent in the Yellow House at Arles. Theo van Gogh guaranteed them 250 francs a month in return for the whole of Vincent's output and one Gauguin canvas. By this means Vincent hoped to rejuvenate his brother's collection with paintings by the artist he so much revered. Their association lasted a brief two months; this was long enough, however, for Vincent to profit by the influence of the man he called the 'chief' of their school, an influence clearly discernible in this perhaps unfinished picture.

198

VINCENT VAN GOGH (1853–1890)　　　　　November 1888
THE WALK (RECOLLECTIONS OF THE GARDEN AT ETTEN)　　Oil on canvas
Catalogue No. 9116　　　　　　　　　　　　Height 73.5 cm. (29″)
　　　　　　　　　　　　　　　　　　　Width 92.5 cm. (36½″)

At Pont Aven, Gauguin expressed the opinion that Vincent was still 'up to his ears in Neo-Impressionism and floundering considerably'. He proceeded to reveal to him the new aesthetic principles. This picture, for example, was inspired by Gauguin's 'Women in a garden, Arles', an audacious and satirical picture in a bolder vein. Van Gogh remains more sensitive. 'Gauguin', he said, 'gives me the courage to imagine things, and certainly things from the imagination take on a more mysterious character.'

Formerly Schukin Collection.

VINCENT VAN GOGH (1853–1890)
PRISONERS EXERCISING

Oil on canvas
Height 80 cm. (31^1/$_2$″)
Width 64 cm. (25^1/$_4$″)

In any list of Van Gogh's favourite painters we should expect to find the names of Rembrandt, Delacroix and the masters of the Japanese print. Rembrandt 'because he penetrates so deeply into the mysterious that he says things which no language can ever express'; Delacroix because it is to him we owe the lesson of 'arbitrary colouring'; and the Japanese masters because it is they who inspire 'the desire to paint with ease, as if it were all as simple as buttoning up one's waistcoat'. We are not surprised to find there the artists of the Golden Age of the Dutch landscape, and Frans Hals; and it seems only natural that he should have admired Jules Dupré ('a true brother of Delacroix'), Millet ('an example to young painters in every field') and those painters whom he considered as his earliest masters: Mauve and Israëls. All his life he was haunted by Monticelli, the master colourist, who died insane. More difficult to understand is his passion for contemporary realist painters, or the mannerist Meissonnier.

When, in 1889, Vincent was confined in the asylum at St Remy de Provence, he was short of subjects, and, knowing that he would soon exhaust the supply of models in the form of doctors and warders, he asked Theo for more prints. He painted after Lavieille and Millet, and dreamed of transposing into colour the woodcuts of Daumier and Régamy. 'Working thus on drawings and woodcuts is not simply copying,' he wrote to Theo, 'it is more like translating into another language, that of colour, the impressions of light and shade and black and white.' He drew up for himself a long work programme, so that, as he concluded 'even half shut up as I am I shall be able to keep myself occupied for a long time.' Whatever the outcome he feared, Van Gogh never envisaged the possibility that he might cease to paint. Even if he could no longer leave the asylum he would make copies or rather 'translations' in which he could express himself completely; for, except for the subject, certain details of composition and the technique of parallel strokes – perhaps inspired by the hatchings of the wood engraving – this work retains nothing of the spirit of Gustave Doré. The broken tortured line belongs to Van Gogh alone, and none but he would have imagined the subtle contrasts of the blue and ochre stones building up the silence overhanging the shuffling of the convicts, in whom the painter may well have recognized something of his own sad state.

Morosov Collection; at present in the Pushkin Museum, Moscow.

VINCENT VAN GOGH (1853–1890)   1888
THE RED VINEYARD, ARLES   Oil on canvas
                                         Height 73 cm. (28³/₄″)
                                          Width 92 cm. (36¹/₄″)

Van Gogh was not convinced by his 'synthetist' experiments. 'I messed
up the thing I did of the garden at Etten, and I feel that, for works of
the imagination, a certain amount of habit is required,' he told his brother.
Van Gogh was thus more than ever convinced of the importance of 'suggestive colour', which distinguished him from the Impressionists. Still in
company with Gauguin, he set to work on portraits and landscapes, seeking
to express in colour more than had ever been expressed before.

    Formerly Morosov Collection; at present in the Pushkin Museum, Moscow.

VINCENT VAN GOGH (1853–1890)   1890
AUVERS LANDSCAPE IN THE RAIN   Oil on canvas
Height 72 cm. (28³/₈″)
Width 90 cm. (35¹/₂″)

During the last two months of his life Van Gogh painted 70 pictures at
Auvers, a favourite spot for painters. Some of them, ('Cornfield with
ravens') show clearer signs than any of his previous works of the tragedy
then threatening his genius. The landscape reproduced here is, on the
contrary, strangely calm. Perhaps the rain, rediscovered this spring after
years of Provençal sunshine, had brought a brief respite. This picture of
the Auvers fields is a peaceful, rational work superimposed for a moment
on the quivering, reeling world which Van Gogh carried within him.

Formerly Morosov Collection; at present in the Pushkin Museum, Moscow.

PAUL GAUGUIN (1848–1903) 1891, Tahiti
Te Tiare Farani Oil on canvas
Height 73 cm. (28³/₄″)
Width 92 cm. (36¹/₄″)

Gauguin at 43, anxious to get away, felt that he needed the East in order
to 'steep myself anew, to gain new strength from contact with its soil'. The
triumph of the Impressionists, which he felt to be imminent, the facility
with which he was able to apply the principles of Synthetism (and the
growing tendency to regard him as a follower of Bernard and Serusier) – all
this contributed to a realization of his spiritual solitude. This picture with
Gauguin's favourite contrast of faces and still-lifes was painted to forget all
this. Only the faintest echo of Cézanne remains.

Formerly Morosov Collection; at present in the Pushkin Museum, Moscow.

PAUL GAUGUIN (1843–1903)
NATIVITY
Catalogue No. 6568

1896, Tahiti
Oil on canvas
Height 66 cm. (26")
Width 75 cm. (29¹/₂")

One of the first works with which Gauguin declared himself satisfied in
Tahiti was the famous 'Ia Orana Maria' (Hail Mary). Although passionately
interested in the native religion, he painted a number of works of Christian
inspiration while in the Islands. Gauguin was no more a religious painter
in Tahiti than he had been in Pont Aven. He was simply attracted by the
idea of a Maori Virgin, Child or Angel.

PAUL GAUGUIN (1848–1903)　　　　　　　　　　　　　1892, Tahiti
Aha oe feii? What, Are You Jealous?　　　　　　　　　Oil on canvas
　　　　　　　　　　　　　　　　　　　　　　　　Height 66 cm. (26″)
　　　　　　　　　　　　　　　　　　　　　　Width 89 cm. (35¹/₄″)

This is one of Gauguin's most beautiful works, revealing both his maturity
and his independence. He is no longer indebted to anyone, neither to
Impressionist nor Synthetist. 'You know,' he wrote to Monfreid, 'people
try to saddle me with a system, whereas in point of fact I have none at
all. I paint as I please; light one day, dark the next. If an artist is not
free, then he is no artist.' Gauguin has here harmonized his two figures,
one of them being the prolongation in light of the darker. The two arms
creating a single erotic form are re-echoed in the coloured patterns on the
left and the rhythm of the leaves above the bronzed, sunlit flesh.

　　Formerly Schukin Collection; at present in the Pushkin Museum, Moscow.

206

PAUL GAUGUIN (1848–1903)   1891, Tahiti
Parau, parau. Conversation   Oil on canvas
Catalogue No. 8980   Height 62.5 cm. (24¹/₂″)
                                                Width 92.5 cm. (36¹/₂″)

In Brittany, Gauguin's women were always busy making hay or tending the
cows. His Tahitian women are subject to no such necessities; they are
beautiful and that suffices. He seeks to express this Paradise Regained in
the grouping of the figures scattered over his landscapes. At the same time
he feels less and less obliged to tell a story; he paints simply men and
women, standing, sitting, lying. In form, they resemble certain of his Breton
women, for he had already expressed the harmony of man with earth and
its beasts in his Breton picture of 1891, 'The awakening of spring'. What
is new is the freedom, facility and spontaneity.

   Formerly Morosov Collection.

PAUL GAUGUIN (1848–1903)   1894, Paris?
NAVE, NAVE MOE: THE SPRING OF DELIGHT   Oil on canvas
Catalogue No. 6510   Height 73 cm. (28³/₄")
                                              Width 98 cm. (38³/₄")

'In painting as in music, the artist should seek to suggest rather than to
describe. People call me incomprehensible because they are always trying
to find in my pictures an expository aspect which they do not posses,' wrote
Gauguin to Monfreid. The keynote of this picture is a religious sense of
beauty; the scene depicted – dancing before statues of the Moon Gods.
On the brink of the Spring of Delight the admirable nude figure already seen
in 'Aha oe Feii?' sits sunning herself against a Tahitian background in which
nature assumes dreamlike colours. Everything here is strange: the flowers
become arabesques, just as Hokusai's waterfalls become veined marble.
    Formerly Morosov Collection.

208

PAUL GAUGUIN (1848–1903)
Rupe, rupe: Fruit Gathering

1899, Tahiti
Oil on canvas
Height 130 cm. (51¼″)
Width 190 cm. (76″)

The great picture, 'What are we, whence come we and whither go we?',
painted by Gauguin in 1897 just before he made an unsuccessful attempt to
kill himself, left him with a taste for vast compositions in which figures
predominate over landscape. This picture was his attempt to resolve the
doubts which had beset him since his return to Tahiti. Gauguin is now
dedicated to simplicity. He has renounced stylised ornamentation. Monfreid
was requested to stop exhibiting his pictures. Gauguin no longer had anything at all in common with his contemporaries. There is no 'theory' behind
his line of three figures beside the closed circle formed by the bending
horseman and the suckling bitch. This is an unpretentious picture; monumental, classical, perfect. Three months after Gauguin's death, Monfreid,
believing him alive, wrote to tell him that a collector had offered 3,300
francs for this canvas and two others.

Formerly Schukin Collection; at present in the Pushkin Museum, Moscow.

PAUL GAUGUIN (1848–1903) 1899. Tahiti
TE AVAE NO MARIA *(Tahitian Woman with Flowers)* Oil on canvas
Catalogue No. 6515 Height 94 cm. (37")
Width 72 cm. (28¼")

This may be either a study for the preceding picture, or a detail from it selected for further treatment. Gauguin frequently analysed and reassembled components in this way, and in many of his works we find different arrangements of the same figures, in the same postures. Thus in 'Rupe, Rupe' we recognize not only the figure in the picture here reproduced, but also one of those in 'Tahitian women with bare breasts', where the translucence of the breasts contrasts with the brilliance of the red flowers clasped against them, as well as one of those riders on the beach whom Gauguin, during this period of his career, was in the habit of painting. Gauguin was working inside his hut, leaving it to return to the study of his subject only when he felt the need to confirm or correct the way in which he had rendered it. This studio work differentiates him completely from his Impressionist seniors and even from Cézanne, who was always advising his young colleagues to 'look at nature'. It is perhaps paradoxical to say that Gauguin, the great traveller, was probably of all the artists of his day the one who least needed 'to see the world'. In Oceania as in Brittany, he remained always a visionary, in search neither of the exotic nor of the satisfactions of the accurate reporter. But in Tahiti and in the Marquesas, far from the artistic coteries of Paris and from domestic ties more sharply felt in Europe, he found an atmosphere of beauty and of freedom, in which he felt able to expand. This is clearly visible in 'Te avae no Maria', which portrays a woman with flowers in her hands, a tall, slender, supple, figure with the far-away look of some Botticelli Venus.

Where did she come from? Perhaps Gauguin came upon her outlined against some sinuous stream of sunlight, flowing down between the leaves, the fruits and their shadows. 'Shadows' is perhaps hardly the right word, for in Gauguin's pictures there are no shadows, but only colour, even as in Elysium itself the souls are shadowless. It is more probably that it was in his own particular Paradise that Gauguin found her, endowing her with the shapes of imagination, the lines of memory, the colours and the mystery of dreams. Measured in ordinary terms of space, his pictures are not accurate. Their truth is of another order; its reality, no doubt echoed by the dazzling Tahitian sun, was contained within the painter himself: a secret truth, a dream of happiness, the peaceful world of the true Gauguin.

Formerly Schukin Collection.

210

CAMILLE PISSARO (1830–1903)
PLACE DU THÉÂTRE FRANÇAIS, PARIS
Catalogue No. 6509

1898
Oil on canvas
Height 65.5 cm. (25³/₄″)
Width 81.5 cm. (32¹/₄″)

'Looking at his art as a whole, we find, in spite of its fluctuations, not only an extremely strong and consistent artistic purpose but also an essentially intuitive and thoroughbred art. But Pissarro, you may object, borrowed from everyone. Well, why not? Everyone has borrowed from him too, only they will not admit it. As far as I am concerned, I freely admit that he was one of my masters.' It is Gauguin writing of Pissarro, whose work represents a link between Corot and modern art.

Formerly Schukin Collection.

212

PAUL CÉZANNE (1839–1906)   1867–69
GIRL AT THE PIANO   Oil on canvas
Catalogue No. 9166   Height 57 cm. (22¹/₂")
                                                     Width 92 cm. (36¹/₄")

The name of Paul Cézanne is, of course, inseparable from that of the
Impressionist movement. He consorted with its masters, he exhibited his
pictures side by side with theirs. And yet, apart from the landscapes painted
between 1873 and 1878, his whole work was a negation of Impressionist
principles. When Cézanne painted this picture he had already known Manet,
Renoir, Pissarro, Monet and Sisley for some ten years. In 1861 he had been
drawing in the company of Pissarro and Guillaumin. Apparently unaffected
by this propinquity, however, he was producing erotico-romantic compositions. At that time Cézanne painted from his imagination, passionately,
lyrically and without method. The picture here reproduced, together with
certain other still-lifes and portraits must be accounted as one of his first
'reasoned' efforts. It is a strange work, foreshadowing the vivid décors of
Matisse. Yet we find the use of colour and ornamentation less interesting than
the way in which the artist is beginning to construct his volumes.
    Formerly Morosov Collection.

PAUL CÉZANNE (1839–1906)   1890
STILL LIFE WITH A SUGAR BOWL   Oil on canvas
Height 61 cm. (24″)
Width 90 cm. (35¹/₂″)

Here we have the epitome of all Cézanne's still-lifes: the kitchen table, the
cloth which enfolds the inevitable apples, jug and sugar bowl – all the
dramatis personae in the action which the artist was to depict throughout
his career. For action it is, and action of the utmost subtlety. It requires all
the genius of Cézanne to interest us in a collection of such ordinary
objects. With what infinite patience he investigates the shape of each piece
of fruit, each fold of linen! This picture is a symphony of rhythmic ovals
and circles within a diagonal framework imposed by the lines which,
springing from the base of the unexpected little pedestal table high on the
right, range down to the firm horizontal lines of the main table. The cloth
adds a degree of fluidity to an otherwise rigid composition. Never since
Da Vinci has art been so clearly '*cosa mentale*'.
    Formerly Morosov Collection; at present in the Pushkin Museum, Moscow.

PAUL CÉZANNE (1839–1906)   1888
BANKS OF THE MARNE   Oil on canvas
Catalogue No. 6513   Height 65 cm. (25¹/₂″)
                                       Width 81 cm. (32″)

Cézanne may have chosen this particular subject because the landscape
and its double in the water was the Impressionist motif par excellence, and
because he wished to paint it in his own particular way – which was the
antithesis of Impressionism. Instead of seeking the iridescence of the
reflection, he looks for a succession of architectural forms. The river does
not reflect the house and trees very strongly, and the scene in the water
is rather a distant reverberation than an echo of the model.
    Formerly Morosov Collection.

PAUL CÉZANNE (1839–1906)   1888. Paris
MARDI GRAS   Oil on canvas
                                                    Height 102 cm. (39³/₄")
                                                     Width 81 cm. (32")

The Mardi Gras seems an unexpected subject for Cézanne. He is surely the last artist one would expect to paint a scene such as that of Pierrot playing some trick behind the back of a solemn Harlequin. Mischief is not his line; nor is there any trace of humour in this 'comedy'. Did Cézanne intend to amuse? This picture raises no hint of a smile; conveys no feeling of satire. Does this prove that the artist failed in his true aim; that he produced a masterpiece in a manner that he did not intend? It is widely believed that Cézanne achieved greatness only because he was incapable of academic painting. But it is more probable that he broached the theme of the masquerade in a spirit of curiosity: to try his hand at 'genre' painting. He is known to have been an admirer of Daumier and probably it was the old master himself who inspired him with the idea of costumed figures.

The fact that Cézanne painted a number of Harlequin figures round about this time makes the subject none the less exceptional for him. But this picture had a considerable influence on certain young painters (from Picasso to Derain) who saw it at the Salon d'Automne in 1904. Indeed there are few artists who have not since passed through a 'period' during which the figures of the *Commedia dell' Arte* are to be seen, posing with Cézanne-like gravity. But their only real debt to Cézanne is the outward appearance of these figures, Pierrot's empty eyes, Harlequin's mask-like face.

As for Cubism, Cézanne has retained only the design: pick out the various cones, spheres and cylinders in this picture, observe how they fit together, and you will see that this Mardi Gras is a truly Cubist composition. The Cubists, however, were no longer looking for that hard-won harmony of form and subject which gives this Mardi Gras its moving, rough-hewn character. The curtains are not flying in the wind, they are volumes and colours resembling curtains. Similarly the hands of the figures are primarily forms and values resembling hands: and not always even that, for Pierrot's left hand is no more than a token and Harlequin's right more like a glove than a hand. Thus Cézanne's art achieved its greatness in a kind of ambiguity. The painter knew himself to be inimitable: 'Since my work springs from my personal sensations,' he wrote, 'I fail to see how anyone else can fathom it.'

Formerly Schukin Collection: at present in the Pushkin Museum, Moscow.

216

PAUL CÉZANNE (1839–1906)   1898–1902
ROAD NEAR MONT SAINTE-VICTOIRE Oil on canvas
Catalogue No. 8991   Height 78 cm. (30³/₄″)
          Width 99 cm. (39″)

Cézanne, basing his art on his personal reactions to colour, what he called
his 'sensations colorantes', never imitated nature, but set himself to recreate
its mechanisms. Nothing could be more audacious than this portrait of a
mountain, this great upward thrust of rock into a heavy, tortured sky high
above the taut, swift curves cut by the road and the big tree in the foreground. Here, Cézanne is giving free rein to the dynamism which charac-
terized his earliest work but was for a long time held in check: at the age
of sixty, he has regained the ardour of his youth.

 Formerly Morosov Collection.

PAUL CÉZANNE (1839–1906) 　　　　　　　　　　1890–94
THE BATHERS 　　　　　　　　　　　　　　　　Oil on canvas
　　　　　　　　　　　　　　　　　　　Height 26 cm. (10¹/₄″)
　　　　　　　　　　　　　　　　　　　Width 40 cm. (15³/₄″)

Painting nude figures from life on the banks of the River Arc was one of
Cézanne's dreams and even as late as 1904 he confessed to being tempted
when someone offered to pose for him by the riverside. In all his work no
subject is richer or more characteristic than that of the bather. One of the
sketches which he sent to his friend Zola in 1859 showed his youthful friends
splashing beneath the trees. But whereas in his pictures of 1865 he painted
bodies intertwined against a brilliant sky, and in 1875 was still preoccupied
with 'the love struggle', little by little he was to shed his eroticism, and
open-air nudes came to represent for him a subject of exactly the same
order as apples on a plate. And yet this picture, like the other bathing
scenes, must be counted among the artist's most lyrical works; showing a
pure, unsensual lyricism, an expression of pure, superbly modelled joy.

　　Formerly Morosov Collection: at present in the Pushkin Museum, Moscow.

PAUL CÉZANNE (1839–1906)   1897–1900
Pine-Trees and Aqueduct (The Viaduct)   Oil on canvas
                                                     Height 91 cm. (36″)
                                                     Width 71 cm. (28″)

Seven trees in a plain – a picture not unlike certain Poussin drawings. And, indeed, Cézanne lived with a classical landscape always before his eyes. But the relationship between the two painters goes deeper than a mere affinity in the choice of subject. In both we find the same reconstruction of the world, the same work process which, taking as its starting point some tree or fruit, seems to take us straight to the very mainspring of the universe – a strange yet logical experience, since perfection and mystery go hand in hand. The surprising element in this picture is the tree which divides the composition into two parts, and does not even seem to be a tree at all until we discover its crowning tuft of greenery. It is an axis rather than a tree, the axis of the picture itself, a vertical line dropping sheer down to the horizontal plane of reds and greens, knotted like a rock in the centre. The little clump of trees is set round this axis. In the background runs the viaduct (or aqueduct) and the mountain beyond is the Mont Sainte-Victoire. The perfection of this composition is due less to nature than to the artist, now confident enough to transgress all the most elementary rules of politeness towards nature, since his own homage is far greater than the passing nod usually accorded to the line of the horizon by painters more conventional than he. Here the green line which prolongs the viaduct at the foot of the mountain even cuts into one of the foreground trees, and the greens splashed round the central pine tree have been given the same tone values as those much further in the background. We see clearly here how Cézanne built up his landscapes, basing them on immediate sensory values and not on an empirical knowledge of the world. By means of his lights and darks, his colours which express light and space, Cézanne sought to discover the basic emotional pattern of every subject he painted. Thus in this picture, wedged firmly between two right angles, towering above a foreground constructed on the stability of complementary values, and above a calm, classical horizon, he presents a furious outburst of pine branches against a blue sky, and the Provencal landscape becomes a burst of celestial violence above a peaceful earth.

Formerly Schukin Collection: at present in the Pushkin Museum, Moscow.

PAUL CÉZANNE (1839–1906)   c. 1900–1904
WOMAN IN BLUE   Oil on canvas
Catalogue No. 8890   Height 88.5 cm. (32½")
Width 72 cm. (28¼")

This picture is characteristic of Cézanne's maturity. The treatment has
become considerably more free. The figure work is no longer laboured and,
in spite of its extremely precise construction, the painting has a vibrant
quality. Is this a finished picture? Cézanne would often return to a canvas,
but this one appears to be perfectly worked out. If the hands are only
roughed in, it is because the painter did not wish to distract attention from
the face. As for the face itself, he has endowed it with just enough life
to ensure that it is not mistaken for plaster. We have here the portrait
of an utterly joyless, lifeless creature dressed in her Sunday best. This
worthy provincial lady, in her remarkable hat, is generally identified as
Madame Cézanne herself, née Hortense Fiquet. But whilst this picture may
be an accurate portrait of a singularly unobtrusive woman, it is also an
extremely powerful work of art.

Cézanne once gave the following advice to a young painter: 'Get to
the heart of what you see, and then try to express what you feel about it
as logically as you can.' Nothing could be clearer: the painter's first duty
is to express himself. But Cézanne is even more specific: 'The most important
thing is theory – theory developed and applied while actually experiencing
the closest possible contact with nature.' This interchange, this inner struggle
gives his painting its characteristic tension. This portrait, for instance, is
constructed on a series of closely related triangles suggested by the form of
the model herself; by her posture, by the shape of her dress lapels. But
the subject must also conform to a pattern, and it is at this point that the
picture begins to show those plastic 'adjustments' which make Cézanne's
painting at once so disciplined and so free. The three-legged table in the
still-life and the great, light pine tree of the 'Viaduct' have already provided
illustrations: here it is the angle on the left of the picture, re-echoing the
leaning arm and the highly coloured values of the table cloth, which place
the model within the solid framework of a paralellogram.

However, Cézanne cannot be reduced to terms of geometry. In his
opinion 'a sense of art' was more important than a talent for harmony or
colouring.

Formerly Schukin Collection.

222

PAUL SIGNAC (1863–1935)
The Bertaud Pine-Tree

c. 1899
Oil on canvas
Height 73 cm. (28³/₄")
Width 92 cm. (36¹/₄")

Signac liked to paint the giant umbrella pines that are still a feature of the bay of St Tropez. This picture is contemporaneous with the publication of his book *From Delacroix to Neo-Impressionism*. In this work, after paying tribute to his predecessors, he expounds the ideas which, since the exhibition of Seurat's 'Summer Sunday at La Grande Jatte' (1886), had caused a certain number of painters to take 'Divisionism' as their point of departure – that is, they applied their paint in such a way that the primary colours combined in the spectator's eye to form the desired tones.

Formerly Schukin Collection: at present in the Pushkin Museum, Moscow.

PAUL SIGNAC (1863–1935)
MARSEILLES
Catalogue No. 6524

c. 1906
Oil on canvas
Height 46 cm. (18″)
Width 55 cm. (21¹/₂″)

Divisionism had wide repercussions not only on the contemporaries of Seurat and Signac but also on their juniors. Matisse and the Fauves, in particular, all went through a Divisionist period; but only Signac the originator of the theory, remained faithful to it. The idea was Seurat's, but Signac formulated it. He must have found it a useful check on his ardent nature which might have led him into the realms of pure effusion and disorder.

Formerly Morosov Collection.

HENRI ROUSSEAU (1844–1910)
Tropical Forest
Catalogue No. 6536

Oil on canvas
Height 46 cm. (18″)
Width 55 cm. (21½″)

The tropical forest is a recurrent theme in Rousseau's work. The flora he depicts botanists identify as French rather than tropical – and sometimes flowering only in the artist's fertile imagination. This picture demonstrates Rousseau's technique, which, unlike that of many Primitives, is strong, abundant and extremely bold. Ostensibly old-fashioned, the naïve Rousseau is, all the same, a modern painter.

Formerly Schukin Collection.

HENRI ROUSSEAU (1844–1910)   1909

CHOPIN'S MONUMENT IN THE LUXEMBOURG GARDENS, PARIS   Oil on canvas

Catalogue No. 7716   Height 38 cm. (15")

                                                        Width 47 cm. (19¹/₄")

Rousseau painted Paris at the turn of the century. Not the Paris of Degas
and Toulouse-Lautrec, but a worthy, petit-bourgeois city of tall, narrow
houses. This corner of the Luxembourg gardens, with Dubois' monument
to Chopin, has not been touched to this day, but it must be admitted that
it never possessed the strange nobility which here transforms a public garden
into a dream garden. This work is dated 1909, the year in which Uhde
organized the first private exhibition of Rousseau's work.

Formerly Schukin Collection.

PIERRE BONNARD (1867–1947)   1911
MORNING IN PARIS   Oil on canvas
Catalogue No. 9107   Height 76.5 cm. (30″)
                                                      Width 122 cm. (47″)

Morosov had a penchant for Bonnard's work and commissioned him to
paint, for his Moscow town house, a series of three large panels on a
Mediterranean theme. Among other pictures he bought from Bonnard
were these two Parisian scenes, which rank among the artist's finest works.
The comparison between morning and evening in Paris demonstrates no
doubt the persistence of the Impressionist atmosphere, but the composition
is remarkably dynamic; his 'Morning' possesses an intrinsic vitality on
every plane. The blend of precision and mistiness in 'Evening' follows the
golden rule of Verlaine and the Symbolist poets: the broken lines of the
figures darken towards the base of the picture while the tall houses are
already bathed in mist. In this picture the eye juggles with pieces of cab,
scraps of dog, slices of girl, fragments of street-hawker, all of which contribute to a 'slice of life' in a truly cinematographic framework.
  Formerly Morosov Collection.

228

PIERRE BONNARD (1867–1947)　　　　　　　　　1911
Evening in Paris　　　　　　　　　　　　　　Oil on canvas
Catalogue No. 9105　　　　　　　　Height 76 cm. (29³/₄")
　　　　　　　　　　　　　　　　　　Width 121 cm. (46³/₄")

Complained Sérusier of some of the Nabis within ten years of their forma-
tion: 'I protested against the individualism which has become the basis of
their art. But have they given this matter a thought since then? I have no
way of knowing.' Probably not, since the Nabi group was a union of two
tendencies, one (that of Paul Sérusier) considering Gauguin as the founder
of a mystic art, the other wanting to take from the master only his lesson of
absolute freedom. But this basically divided movement may have left a
deeper mark on certain of its nembers than did more strictly formal
groupings such as those of the Cubists and the Fauves. A certain 'family
resemblance' persisted for some time between Bonnard, Vuillard, Valloton
and even Denis. This may have been due to their approach to life, to the
curiosity about their contemporaries which made them the true descendants
of Renoir, Monet, Degas and Toulouse-Lautrec.
　　Formerly Morosov Collection.

229

EDOUARD VUILLARD (1868–1940)   Oil on canvas
INDOOR SCENE WITH CHILDREN   Height 83 cm. (32¹/₄″)
Width 74 cm. (29¹/₈″)

This work is radiantly simple. If the children were more static and the scene beyond the balcony more sharply defined we might well attribute it to Matisse and date it, at will, anywhere between 1905 and 1920. But while Vuillard did share Matisse's feeling for colour and tried, like Matisse, to paint 'a flat surface covered with colours assembled in a given order', he did not share this artist's aesthetic curiosity. As early as 1895 he had abandoned the path of artistic experiment, no longer experiencing the restlessness which lies at the root of the striking contrasts in the works of a Derain or a Picasso. Though welcomed into the Nabi circle by Sérusier, their austerity was not at all in Vuillard's line; he was soon alienated by the theoretical tendencies of the group and became, of all his contemporaries, the artist who best fulfilled the conventional duties of his profession. Vuillard was a true painter of his era, catering for the taste of his admirers and painting society as it actually was during the first decades of this century – that is to say, the ladies in their drawing rooms, the writers, statesmen, artists, business men, surgeons, actors, musicians, each portrayed in his own setting, engaged on his own particular activity: the lady at the telephone, the surgeon at the operating table, the poetess composing in her bed, the couturière among her lengths of cloth. Turning from this portrait of society to the life of the streets, we find, instead of a street conjured up by the imagination of a poet, a specific square or cross-roads; the terrace of a specific café or a passing bus of such and such a line. And Vuillard's métro is not just any métro, but the Villiers métro station. He also painted the theatre of his day, both as scenarist at the Théâtre de l'Oeuvre and as a painter of actors during an actual performance.

Vuillard stands alone in the history of contemporary painting, speaking for a society already slightly out of date, whereas his friend Bonnard appealed to the curiosity of the younger generation. Yet behind the apparent intellectual serenity of Vuillard lay a ceaseless effort and a highly unacademic work process. Beneath a glittering exterior, we find the restless soul of an artist deeply involved with his own times.

At present in the Pushkin Museum, Moscow.

ALBERT MARQUET (1875–1947)
THE PORT OF HONFLEUR

1907–11
Oil on canvas
Height 65 cm. (25¹/₂")
Width 82 cm. (32³/₈")

In 1907 Charles-Louis Philippe had already noted that Marquet possessed a 'balanced view of things which stops him from embarking on unfortunate adventures and keeps him out of trouble'. Yet he was once one of the boldest of the so-called 'roaring' Fauves, and from the year 1897, when he began to study with Matisse, Camoin, Manguin and Rouault in Gustave Moreau's studio, he was one of the first to make use of pure, flat tones. When Matisse and Derain embraced Divisionism, Marquet chose to turn his steps more and more in the direction of delicacy and of moderation.

Formerly Schukin Collection: at present in the Pushkin Museum, Moscow.

ALBERT MARQUET (1875–1947)   1909
THE PORT OF HAMBURG   Oil on canvas
Catalogue No. 8907   Height 68 cm. (26³/₄″)
            Width 81 cm. (32″)

Although a great traveller, Marquet was no seeker after the exotic: he would go as willingly to Le Havre as to Norway. His travels took him to Tangier, Rotterdam, Algiers, Oslo, Assuan, Vigo, the Soviet Union, Venice, Stockholm, Lausanne, Rumania and Hamburg (where this seascape was painted) as often as to the Seine basin. We cannot even be sure that he was looking for a change of atmosphere. He seems rather to have sought a new setting for his perennial subjects: rivers, beaches, harbours.

  Formerly Schukin Collection.

ALBERT MARQUET (1875–1947)　　　　　　　　　　1912
THE PONT SAINT-MICHEL, PARIS　　　　　　　　　Oil on canvas
　　　　　　　　　　　　　　　　　　　　Height 64 cm. (25¼″)
　　　　　　　　　　　　　　　　　　　　Width 80 cm. (31½″)

In France, Marquet lived always by the Seine. From all the various Paris
quarters he occupied the river was never out of sight; he could paint
it by day or by night, in sunshine or in snow, in calm or in flood. This
particular picture was painted from his apartment on the floor above
Matisse, at 19, Quai St Michel. For Matisse the same subject served only as a
springboard, and the street scene became simply the excuse for an interplay
of coloured blobs.

At present in the Pushkin Museum, Moscow.

234

ALBERT MARQUET (1875–1947)   1909
NAPLES   Oil on canvas
Catalogue No. 9150   Height 61.5 cm. (24¼")
Width 80 cm. (31½")

It has been said of Marquet that he painted gaps and that his canvases are merely a series of blanks. True, he was the only artist to paint the shimmering void of a sheet of water and to succeed in bringing it to life by subtle harmonies. His pictures are painted only for the most discerning eyes; those who look at them perfunctorily will see only their monotony. Finding that his glittering colours did not capture light, Marquet turned his gaze full on the sun itself; and from that moment onward all his pictures were painted, as it were, against the light, in a world in which slender silhouettes stand out against the full reverberation of pure light.

Formerly Morosov Collection.

ANDRÉ DÉRAIN (1880–1954)   c. 1907–9
Mountain Road   Oil on canvas
Catalogue No. 9126   Height 80.5 cm. (31³/₄")
                                              Width 99 cm. (39")

'I can see no future for anything but composition, for when I paint from
life I must come to terms with so many trivialities that I lack spontaneity.'
'There is only one kind of painting and that is landscape painting, which
is also the most difficult. Composition is much easier because no one can
prevent each one of us from imagining the world which suits us best.'
(Letters to Vlaminck). These quotations reveal the dilemma facing Dérain.
In the end, like Marquet, he found Fauvism to be untenable.

   Formerly Morosov Collection.

236

ANDRE DERAIN (1880–1954)   c. 1906
The Port of Le Havre   Oil on canvas
Catalogue No. 6540   Height 59 cm. (23¹/₄″)
                          Width 73 cm. (28³/₄″)

In addition to their search for the most direct possible form of expression, the aim of the Fauves was progressive simplification. 'Even in the best of present-day paintings,' wrote Derain to Vlaminck, 'there is one thing which is really important, and a great many others of no basic interest. How much better if they were eliminated.' And so Derain simplified his pictures more and more. For all its scintillation, this is a highly classical painting, in which the simplest of lines is painted with a minimum of colour.

    Formerly Schukin Collection.

ANDRÉ DÉRAIN (1880–1954)
THE CASTLE

c. 1912
Oil on canvas
Height 100 cm. (39³/₈")
Width 65 cm. (25³/₄")

This picture marks a turning-point in the work of Derain, for it still retains something of Cézanne's strictness and yet has left its sources far behind; the painter is now completely free. It indicates the future course of Derain's artistic career; the career of an independent who judged and found wanting all the aesthetic adventures with which he had been involved or merely associated. He once referred to Fauvism as 'an art for dyers' and to Cubism, in a letter to Vlaminck, as 'an idiotic idea'.

Art historians have wondered what drove him to these violent switches. Perhaps the answer lies in Derain's determination to be on his own. There comes a time when a man must break with all schools, even unofficial ones, and with all groups, even those formed by his friends. In making this breakaway Derain turned to the Roman muralists, the Florentine painters, the Faiyum portraitists, and drew upon his memories of negro art. Poussin, Corot, everyone was grist to his mill. The almost monastic starkness and austerity of this period of disintoxication was followed by a period during which Derain attained a masterly virtuosity in an art which was both rustic and sophisticated, the equivalent of what might almost be called, in the language of the interior decorator, 'classical country house'. Derain was a writer as well as a painter, and considered the theatre a means of expression more complete than painting. It is possible that his return to Neo-Classicism was guided by the writings of those authors to whom the experiments of the avant-garde painters and poets were just so much nonsense, and who preached instead the virtues of simplicity. Derain, of course, created the stage sets for Paul Claudel's 'L'Annonce faite à Marie'. And those of Derain's pictures which are in the U.S.S.R. – like 'Saturday' or 'Le Chevalier X' – show a naïve strength and simplicity which call to mind both Claudel and the plays of Jacques Copeau. Our century offers no stranger artistic phenomenon than the painting of Derain. The careers of certain avant-garde artists embrace 40 or 50 years of aesthetic experiment. Derain's career is just as comprehensive, but his sources lie always in the past. It is rarely that we see a Derain without wondering what museum inspired it – and usually concluding that Dérain is even more of an original than one had thought.

Formerly Schukin Collection.

ANDRÉ DÉRAIN (1880–1954)   1913
VIEW OF MARTIGUES, PROVENCE   Oil on canvas
Catalogue No. 9101   Height 140 cm. (55¹/₈")
                                                       Width 89 cm. (35¹/₄")

Derain, after befriending the Cubists, kept Cézanne's severity of form
but nothing of his spirit. Nor did he carry experiment much further. Instead,
after a number of still-lifes and landscapes progressively less and less inspired by Cézanne, he painted pictures like this one where the synthetic
Cubism of the little Provençal village is set in a completely classical landscape. As he himself said: 'The further I go, the more I am alone.'
   Formerly Schukin Collection.

240

ANDRE DERAIN (1880–1954)   c. 1913
The Wood   Oil on canvas
Catalogue No. 9085   Height 116 cm. (43¹/₈″)
                                                      Width 81 cm. (32″)

Derain painted this landscape in his Paris studio. The days of open-air
painting were over. Henceforward, composition was all. But while this
work has its own nobility, it also lacks the spontaneity given by contact
with nature. It has been called classical; but it is not, in fact, modelled on
any one classical period. His painting, whether in his landscapes or his compositions, is a constant re-invention of the classical.
   Formerly Schukin Collection.

HENRI MATISSE (1869–1954) 1908
THE DESSERT, A HARMONY IN RED Oil on canvas
Catalogue No. 9660 Height 180 cm. (71″)
Width 220 cm. (86¹/₂″)

At the Salon d'Automne in 1908, Matisse exhibited a painting called 'The Dessert, a harmony in blue' which was bought by Schukin. But what was delivered was a 'harmony in red'. Matisse had made no changes in the composition; the blue was simply transformed into red, so that the artist might prove to himself his independence in the matter of colour. Henceforward colour is no longer dictated by the objects themselves, but is selected by the painter in direct relationship to what he is seeking to express.

Formerly Schukin Collection.

HENRI MATISSE (1869–1954)
BRONZE FIGURES WITH FRUIT

c. 1909–10
Oil on canvas
Height 90 cm. (35^1/$_2$″)
Width 115 cm. (43^1/$_4$″)

The whole of Matisse is already contained in this still-life, which, though undated, may be placed around 1909 or 1910 since in it we recognize a little bronze modelled by the artist in 1909. This artist frequently made a point of including his own sculptures in his still-life compositions, perhaps challenging himself to include in increasingly 'flat' paintings the solid objects which he himself created. A vertical line and the radiance of the blue background here integrate the forms of his little 'group' into the kaleidoscope of this extremely supple composition. Here, as always with Matisse, subtlety and sensuality are equally blended.

Formerly Schukin Collection: at present in the Pushkin Museum, Moscow.

HENRI MATISSE (1869–1954)
THE GAME OF BOWLS
Catalogue No. 9154

1908
Oil on canvas
Height 113.5 cm. (42³/₄")
Width 145 cm. (55")

This 'Game of bowls' is apparently descended from the celebrated 'Joie de vivre' of 1906, marking Matisse's break with pointillism, but the earlier picture was of a very studied elegance, whereas here we find deliberate simplicity. Matisse wanted to prove that it is possible to paint without observing any of the time-honoured rules. And indeed we soon respond to the counterpoint of the bowls and the black heads of the players; to the brilliant red of the drapery offsetting the weight of the figures on the right. Matisse is here employing a most precise technique.

Formerly Schukin Collection.

244

HENRI MATISSE (1869–1954)
Nymph and Satyr
Catalogue No. 6521

1909
Oil on canvas
Height 89 cm. (35¼")
Width 117 cm. (44")

The theme of this picture, though not surprising, is rare, perhaps indeed unique in the work of Matisse. We have mentioned elsewhere this painter's spontaneous mixture of sensuality and subtlety. Here these qualities are differently combined. The picture, though entitled 'Nymph and Satyr', is far removed from the realms of mythology. The satyr represents the climax of desire. Nor does the artist limit himself to depicting the charms of the flesh: desire is also expressed in the tender curve, threatened by the two slanting lines (the satyr's arms) that seem to hem in the nymph.

Formerly Schukin Collection.

245

HENRI MATISSE (1869–1954)
SPANISH STILL-LIFE
Catalogue No. 6570

c. 1911
Oil on canvas
Height 90 cm. (35¹/₂")
Width 117 cm. (44")

Even the Cubists pay tribute to Matisse. 'It was Matisse', so Ozenfant and
Le Corbusier declared, 'who made Cubism possible.' But it is uncertain
whether Matisse was gratified by such a progeny. After doing so much to
impose his ideas (opening an academy in 1908, publishing in the same year
his theory of art in *Notes d'un peintre*), Matisse abandoned his teaching
and went abroad: to Spain, Moscow and Morocco. He was keeping his
distance from the Parisian mêlée, leaving his juniors to carry yet a stage
further the liberties he had taken. Doubtless he wished to rediscover his art
in works such as this still-life, with its indulgence in arabesques.

Formerly Schukin Collection.

HENRI MATISSE (1869–1954)　　　　　　　　　　　1909
SPANISH WOMAN WITH A TAMBOURINE　　　　　　Oil on canvas
　　　　　　　　　　　　　　　　　　　　　Height 92 cm. (36¹/₄″)
　　　　　　　　　　　　　　　　　　　　　Width 73 cm. (28³/₄″)

The fact that Matisse could paint this costume piece in the same year as the austere 'Game of bowls' demonstrates his complete independence. In direct contrast to the Spanish still-life, painted entirely in the flat, Matisse has here 'modelled' the figure of his Spanish woman, using a deep blue shadow to make it stand out against the paler blue background. This picture is still 'Fauve' – but it is no longer 'roaring' Fauvism.

　　Formerly Schukin Collection: at present in the Pushkin Museum, Moscow.

HENRI MATISSE (1869–1954)　　　　　　　　　　　　　　1910
Music　　　　　　　　　　　　　　　　　　　　　　　Oil on canvas
Catalogue No. 9674　　　　　　　　　　　　　Height 260 cm. (102½″)
　　　　　　　　　　　　　　　　　　　　　Width 389 cm. (153¼″)

Three colours and an outline – in brown for 'The dance' and in black for
'Music': these are the elements Matisse chose for these twin compositions. A
little less still, and 'The dance' might have been entitled 'Tensions', and
'Music' 'Notes upon a stave'. Never again – until his 'paper cut-out' period –
did Matisse dare entrust so much to so little: his subtlety here reaches its
zenith. Just as the scale disappears into supersonic tones unheard by human
ears, so these harmonized lines are the threshold of abstraction. Moreover,
it is not *a* dance but *the* dance, a rising ellipse soaring over what the artist
called a hill, but which is in reality a surface created entirely by the points
of impact, the bounding arcs of this 'architecture' springing from the edges
of the picture.
　　Formerly Schukin Collection.

248

HENRI MATISSE (1869–1954)　　　　　　　　　　　　　1910
THE DANCE　　　　　　　　　　　　　　　　　　Oil on canvas
Catalogue No. 9673　　　　　　　　　　Height 260 cm. (102¹/₂″)
　　　　　　　　　　　　　　　　　　　　　　　Width 391 cm. (154″)

We can imagine the impression made by these two Matisse panels when they
hung on the staircase of Sergei Schukin's eighteenth-century Moscow man-
sion. When he actually saw them in the Salon d'Automne in 1910, the collector had some hesitation in accepting delivery. The nude figures caused
him some disquiet and he subsequently saw to it that the genitals of the male
flute player were masked with a touch of red. 'Imagine the visitor arriving
from outside,' wrote Matisse. 'He sees the first flight of stairs: the effort of
climbing them demands a feeling of release. The first panel therefore represents the Dance, a ring flung over a hilltop. On the second flight one is
inside the house, and here, in harmony with the atmosphere and the silence,
I envisage a musical scene with several listening figures.'
　Formerly Schukin Collection.

HENRI MATISSE (1869–1954)   1909
WOMAN IN GREEN   Oil on canvas
Catalogue No. 6519   Height 65 cm. (25¹/₂″)
                                                 Width 54 cm. (21¹/₄″)

For colour, one small red patch in the centre of a green painting. Matisse
the Fauve has now reached such complete sobriety. The portrait is of Madame Matisse, if 'portrait' indeed is the right term. 'I like Chardin's way
of putting it,' declared Matisse, '"I go on adding colour till I get a
likeness".' Let us then call it a not unrecognisable outline. A few strokes
only have made the face both mysterious and pleasing.
    Formerly Schukin Collection.

HENRI MATISSE (1869–1954)   1910
GIRL WITH TULIPS   Oil on canvas
Catalogue No. 9056   Height 92 cm. (36¹/₄″)
Width 73 cm. (28³/₄″)

Matisse's continual oscillation between various techniques shows that with him doubt often followed upon enthusiasm. For another five or six years he was to continue to explore the possibilities of Cubism and to verge on Abstractionism, before entering on a calmer period. This was abandoned in turn for the mural of 'The dance' (1930) and for the coloured 'paper cut-outs' with which he was to experiment again towards the end of his life.

Formerly Schukin Collection.

251

Oil on canvas
Height 73 cm. (28³/₄")
Width 59.5 cm. (23¹/₂")

Although Impressionism left its mark directly or indirectly on the early works of all the great French painters of the present century, Picasso, for his part, appears to have been oblivious to it. From art school academism he progressed directly towards a satirical style of painting, which makes Degas and Lautrec, who served as his inspiration, appear positively refined. Picasso's art was, at this time, already openly aggressive and very close to Expressionism as it came to flourish at a slightly later date, as in the works of Kirchner. His aim was to caricature. His subjects were those familiar to Rouveyre and other illustrators of reviews. The picturesque fauna of cafés, dance halls, cabarets in which women are clearly recognizable as street-walkers or demi-mondaines, according to the type of establishment and where, as MacOrlan likes to put it, 'pimps are dressed as pimps, employees as employees and slaughterhousemen as slaughterhousemen, all of which is very convenient for draughtsmen on the lookout for "sketches of Parisian life".'

The early Picasso was a virtuoso combining elements of Degas and Lautrec with memories of Van Gogh, a certain Manet-like manual dexterity, and, sometimes even, when the spirit moved him, experiments in pointillism: everything was worth a trial, just to *see*. Picasso had the curiosity of the juggler seeking the ball best suited to his hand.

Hence the importance of this picture, which like the 'Woman drinking absinthe' shows his evolution towards a much stricter and more heavily outlined art (forcing upon him an unaccustomed hieratic discipline which, already popularized by the Synthetists, was by this time in the air), and towards a more limited range of colour. Note, too, the first example of a theme long to remain a favourite: the white-faced Harlequin, much more reminiscent of Banville and Verlaine than of Cézanne. A literary theme, perhaps, for the pre-Cubist Picasso was a sentimental, poetic painter. The Blue Period (of which even his fiercest detractors are willing to make an exception) was imminent, heralded by this picture painted only a month or two earlier. We may thus say that this 'Harlequin', with its already remarkable violence, heralds the revolution which was to enable painting to escape from the conventions of the outdoors and the socially picturesque on which it had been based for 30 years.

Formerly Mo: Collection: at present in the Pushkin Museum, Moscow.

PABLO PICASSO (b. 1881)
THE EMBRACE

c. 1899
Oil on canvas
Height 51.7 cm. (20″)
Width 55.7 cm. (21³/₄″)

Picasso painted this sober picture at the age of nineteen. At this time Matisse was painting landscapes from nature, and still-life studies, as well as compositions like 'The Dessert' which, however bold in conception, are still representational in effect. Bonnard was observing street life, playing with the currently sinuous style. Rouault was taking ever greater liberties with the chiaroscuro he had learnt in art school. Among Picasso's future team-mates, Braque was still engaged on unambitious studies, family portraits and landscapes, Fernand Léger was earning his living as a draughtsman in an architect's office, Villon was working for the illustrated reviews. Picasso had forged ahead, thanks to an artistic precocity which enabled him, at sixteen, to exhibit his portraits in Père Romeu's tavern – a meeting-place for intellectuals in Barcelona – and to win medals in academic competitions. Abandoning the academic path at a very early stage, he began painting and drawing in the streets, in the cafés, in the bull-ring, alternating bulk effects with sharp and satirical Lautrec-like strokes that seize in a single gesture, in no more than a couple of rapid lines, the essential nature of his model. Picasso was a 'brilliant' painter from the very start. In his youth he loved to dazzle by sheer rapidity. Remarkable among so many exercises in virtuosity, this little composition marks a clear-cut evolution towards deliberate sobriety. Picasso's aim was to produce a work, not of style but of the imagination. And while we may smile a little at the thought that this picture marks the true beginning of the future highly abstract master of the 'papiers collés', it also illustrates his remarkably independent mind. A simple picture, but already very free in treatment: we note the skilful flat stroke painting of the woman's skirt, integrated into the volume of the male figure, the relief of the picture concentrated entirely in the arched neck of the lover.

Picasso often returned to the theme of the embrace, for instance in the picture of 1903 where his lovers are naked and the woman pregnant. Here we may note the evolution of the feelings which inspired the artist. The earlier picture is an unserious version of a backstairs love scene. The 1903 painting is a work of great and moving sincerity. However precocious the nineteen-year-old Picasso, he was still merely feeling his way. But he did not have long to wait for his maturity.

Formerly Schukin Collection: at present in the Pushkin Museum, Moscow.

PABLO PICASSO (b. 1881)   1901
PORTRAIT OF JAIME SABARTÈS (LE BOCK)   Oil on canvas
                                                    Height 81.5 cm. (32¼")
                                                       Width 66 cm. (26")

This picture might well be called the portrait of silence. A sober work
–save for the single, almost mannerist, detail of the hand stretched out
along the side of the tankard, – it might be taken for some figure from
Rimbaud's imagination. The same youthfulness, the same finely-chiselled
features contrast with the more rugged volume of the hand. The model was
in fact Sabartès, faithful and probably oldest friend of the painter. The
portrait here shows him more as he must have appeared in his poems than
at the café table. Picasso has shorn the poet of his moustache, removed the
habitual pince-nez and deprived him of the stiff, tubular white collar
normally worn by him and all his contemporaries. Perhaps the loss of his
glasses explains the far-away look in his eyes. Clearly Picasso's aim now
was to find a new style.

Certainly the way in which he has combined an effect of volume with
the deliberate choice of flat tones is surprising. The foreshortening of the
right arm and the summary treatment of the left would no doubt have
startled the masters who had congratulated the young Pablo Ruiz Picasso
on his skill in drawing from classical models and from the nude. Such
simplification is, of course, deliberate.

We do not know whether or not Picasso was impressed by those works
of Cézanne that he probably saw at Vollard's Gallery where, in this same
year, he held his first Paris exhibition. But no traces of their inspiration
are visible in his work. Their rigour, on the other hand, may have stimulated
his desire to reduce the human figure to geometrical forms. The face,
however, and the inspiration of the picture belong to a man unimpressed
by Cézanne's daring experiments. Picasso continues the romantic tradition.
Edvard Munch was the artist whose works were at this time closest to his
own. Moreover, for Picasso, art is not moderation but excess. To the devil
with the Golden Number and perfect equilibrium. What counts is expression. In a Matisse portrait we find harmony; here, contrast. In spite of the
simple rhythms sought by Picasso, this portrait remains that of a young
and disillusioned poet: that is, of a fundamental discord. Hence the expression, in spite of the circle within which a fanatic composition-seeker
might try to inscribe the figure, of prostration, of a fall. The portrait of
silence, as we said before, but also, indubitably, the portrait of despair.

Formerly Schukin Collection: at present in the Pushkin Museum, Moscow.

PABLO PICASSO (b. 1881)   1902
Two Sisters   Oil on wood
Catalogue No. 9071   Height 152 cm. (59³/₄")
                                                Width 100 cm. (39³/₈")

It remained only for Picasso to eliminate the last trace of realism – of the likeness which distinguishes a picture such as the Sabartès portrait – before launching on the creation of his phantom world: a world of blue men and women, draped rather than clothed, suffering for the most part; of guitar players, kerchiefed women and figures so emaciated that their limbs resemble stripped and polished sticks of wood rather than flesh and blood. Much emphasis has been placed on the realism of these pictures, yet, in fact, they are already far removed from realism. These compositions express the poetry of attitudes, gestures and faces of the artist's own creation. Doubtless, there is some echo of El Greco's draped figures, but no trace is to be found of his flamboyant, other-worldly aspect. The memory of Goya may well have encouraged him in the use of monochrome. Probably, too, the pictures of Isidro Nonell, the Barcelona painter of dark sleeping figures dead to the world, of women huddled in their shawls, were not without some influence. But when we look at these compositions as a whole, we see that none of them were ever more than very remote sources of inspiration.

Picasso's art is here right in the tradition of Spanish tragedy: dramatically disembodied and renewed. His figures are indeed the beggars and half-starved women of a poor country. But first and foremost, they belong to a world of dreams engendered by misery but sublimated in the pure monochrome of a blue as untroubled as the sky.

These pictures should not be underestimated. They are sometimes overlooked among Picasso's prodigious output, periods of brilliance being so frequent. We must not forget that this is the voice of a twenty-two-year-old boy, and few painters are insincere at that age. Indeed, it is precisely then that the innermost truth of our nature is most liable to reveal itself. Throughout all the fluctuations of his subsequent career, we find echoes of the note of great nobility that characterizes these early paintings, in the 'Still-life with black bull's head', or in the portraits of Dora Maar and of Jacqueline Z. for instance. This is Picasso's own individual truth: a poignant understanding of the world. The style is deliberately mannerist, but the artist is a virtuoso, oversensitive to human suffering, as skilful in execution as he is divided in soul.

Formerly Schukin Collection.

WOMAN WITH A KERCHIEF   Oil on backed canvas
Catalogue No. 6573   Height 50 cm. (19³/₄")
                                                                Width 36 cm. (14¹/₄")

Picasso began painting at the age of fourteen. By the time he was nineteen he had attained full freedom and was executing highly unacademic sketches of the habitués of the El Quatro Gats Tavern in Barcelona, or recording a corrida in a few swift strokes of pastel. Style came slightly later. From the beginning of his Blue Period (late 1901) he realized the value of discipline, and from this time onwards allowed himself nothing which did not have its place in a logically conceived and organized artistic scheme.

This picture is an essay in precise delineation, without the use of monochrome. Every fold of the blouse has been clearly outlined, not a wrinkle in this hardened, tired, yet youthful face has escaped the painter's brush. The result is a somewhat harsh work, interesting in so far as it reveals the perseverance of an artist who refuses to embark on anything which he is not prepared to carry through to its conclusion.

From this point of view, the work is typical of a period when the artist had no fixed style but was running swiftly through a whole series of styles. Matisse and Léger, also 'forced' their ideas at a similar pace, neither developing a distinctive style until they had completed their experiments.

This portrait is overwhelming from every point of view. Collapse is everywhere. Hair awry, clothes shapeless: it is the portrait of a woman who has exceeded the limits of her strength. True, there is some resemblance to the figures of the Blue Period, but the absence of monochrome, the merciless exactitude of the drawing, deprive it of that element of unreality which rendered the wretched figures of that period so appealing – and so little out of place even amid the elegance of a collector's drawing room. It is possible that Picasso painted this woman because of her likeness to his sad 'blue' women.

Formerly Schukin Collection.

PABLO PICASSO (b. 1881)   1905
MAJORCAN WOMAN   Gouache and watercolour
                                               Height 68 cm. (26³/₄")
                                               Width 52 cm. (20¹/₂")

Mannerism is here predominant. Picasso was always skilful at exploiting
his discoveries. But skill was not enough, he had to delight in them; for
Picasso loved to develop his ideas to the full and to extract from them the
maximum number of pictures. He is after all an extremely practical man.
And so we find here a prolongation of the Blue Period, but in terms of
elegance: a Blue Period taken over by a dress designer or ballet stylist. The
emaciated hand of yesterday is now slender; the heavy draperies have
become an elegant décolleté. The hat adds its own note of 'haute couture',
while the old monochrome treatment has given way to the charm of the
exquisitely fine dialogue of blues and terracottas.

The Pink Period marks Picasso's début as a career painter. The Blue
Period had forced him to reduce to bare essentials an art intended to
appeal to the emotions. Now the aim is to amuse, charm or surprise: free
rein can be given to fantasy. This relaxed mood corresponds to a materially
more prosperous period for the artist. In 1905 he completed the Saltim-
banques series of etchings commissioned by Vollard. Shortly afterwards
Matisse introduced him to Schukin who, within the space of nine years was
to purchase no fewer than fifty of his paintings. Leo and Gertrude Stein
were beginning to champion his work, and in the same year appeared
Guillaume Apollinaire's first article devoted to his painting. With the
Salon d'Automne came the advent of Fauvism. The Salon des Indépendants
gave a retrospective showing of the works of Seurat and Van Gogh. Clearly
Picasso was outside the mainstream of the rising generation of painters, the
painters of whom everyone was talking. The new art was brilliant, un-
bridled, free from all restraint. Picasso, on the sidelines, was defending the
values of sobriety, moderation, and distinction. Their subjects were approximately those of Gauguin: evocations of life in a paradise of sun. Picasso's
world was a cold world of imagination, where strange emaciated figures
huddled in tawdry circus rags. Picasso's circus is far removed from Lautrec's
glittering arena, far removed, indeed, from reality itself. He transposed it
in just the same way as Watteau chose the forest as a setting for his
Commedia dell'Arte figures.

Formerly Schukin Collection: at present in the Pushkin Museum, Moscow.

PABLO PICASSO (b. 1881)
THE DRYAD
Catalogue No. 7704

1908
Oil on canvas
Height 185 cm. (73″)
Width 108 cm. (42¹/₂″)

In the 'Two sisters' of 1902, the eye of the figure on the right is 'written', not represented; the 'Demoiselles d'Avignon' (1906–7), a work of emancipation, also has such 'written' eyes. Not Cubism but primitive and early art inspired this geometrization of expression – negro sculpture, romanesque frescoes. Painted at a time when artists strove to cap novelty with novelty, this 'Dryad' is one of the most balanced and classical of Picasso's works.

Formerly Schukin Collection.

264

PABLO PICASSO (b. 1881)　　　　　　　　　　　　1908
THE HOUSE IN THE GARDEN　　　　　　　　　　　Oil on canvas
Catalogue No. 6533　　　　　　　　　　Height 73 cm. (28³/₄″)
　　　　　　　　　　　　　　　　　　　　Width 61 cm. (24″)

This is no particular house or tree, but the idea of a house, the idea of a tree.
Picasso was emerging from his 'blue' backgrounds in much the same way as
the primitives when they transformed their golden backgrounds into settings
for the Life of Christ or of his Saints. Reversions to earlier styles can be
dangerous. But the example of the primitives did not lead Picasso into
archaist aesthetic theory. Here he chose to use supposedly 'weak' elements.
　Formerly Schukin Collection.

PABLO PICASSO (b. 1881)   1908
Woman with a Fan   Oil on canvas
Catalogue No. 7705   Height 150 cm. (59″)
                                                       Width 100 cm. (39³/₈″)

An enlightening comparison can be made between 'Woman with a fan' and
Renoir's treatment of the same subject. Which is the more revolutionary of
these two paintings? The echoes of the battle over Cubism have long since
died, and Picasso's world is just as accessible as Renoir's. In fact, Picasso's
'Woman with a fan', executed at the very beginning of the Cubist movement,
may today seem to us the more classical of the two.
    Formerly Schukin Collection.

PABLO PICASSO (b. 1881)   1909
QUEEN ISABEAU   Oil on canvas
                                              Height 92 cm. (36¹/₄")
                                              Width 73 cm. (28³/₄")

Again and again Picasso comes back to such motionless figures as this one of
a girl with her eyelids lowered as if in sleep. Why are they so still? Perhaps
because they are listening to the melody of the painting itself, this time
composed exclusively of lightness and grace. Look well at the greenery in
this picture, for Picasso's art is soon to be concentrated on the most arid
forms of Cubism.

Formerly Schukin Collection: at present in the Pushkin Museum, Moscow.

PABLO PICASSO (b. 1881)   1913
VIOLIN AND GLASS   Oil on canvas
                                                     Height 65 cm. (25$^{1}/_{2}$")
                                                     Width 54 cm. (21$^{1}/_{4}$")

Cubism is at its zenith. The laboured details which, under the influence of
Cézanne, had characterised the periods known successively as analytical,
synthetic and hermetic Cubism might suggest that its practitioners were
austere theoreticians, denying themselves most of the joys of painting. But
in 1913, Picasso showed in a series of works such as this 'Violin and glass'
that Cubism in all its orthodoxy had not dried up his artistic sensibility.
Indeed he had never painted with such relish. This period may also be
regarded as a time of stability after a period of experiment during which he
was at last able to exploit to the full the experience he had gained.
There is no more a conflict with reality in this picture; the artist has
retained nothing liable to interfere with his freedom of invention. He has
opened up the violin, removed the strings, extracted the soul and done with
it what he pleased. All restrictions have been cast aside, resulting in absolute
freedom. Picasso thus added a new image to our 'Musée imaginaire'. Henceforward 'Glass and violin', 'Guitar and bottle', 'Pipe and fruit dish' take
their place in the repertory of art side by side with 'Leda and the Swan',
'St George and the Dragon', 'St Antony and his Pig'. Formula rather than
subject, this assembled interplay of planes, among which are scattered the
last allusions to reality, was destined to become a popular artistic theme. But
such allusions are symbols rather than representations, so that the picture
here reproduced retains only a distant echo of music, of the transverse
rhythm of a wrought-iron rail suggesting a balcony, the stem of a glass
recalling some tranquil table. The association of ideas is not difficult and
even if the spectator performs this operation unconsciously, the suggestion
of a musical interlude helps him to appreciate to the full the reassuring
depth and sonority of the picture. This is a work of great freedom, purity
and stability, harmonious in both form and matter. It dates from the
beginning of the first Cubist experiments in 'papiers collés', when the urge
to stick instead of to paint led artists to introduce into their pictures pieces
of mirror, bits of cloth, or grains of sand, Picasso being always ready to
prove himself as bold a sticker as any of the rest.
    Formerly Schukin Collection: at present in the Pushkin Museum, Moscow.

PABLO PICASSO (b. 1881)　　　　　　　　　　　　　　　　1910
PORTRAIT OF AMBROISE VOLLARD　　　　　　　　　　　Oil on canvas
Height 93 cm. (36³/₄″)
Width 66 cm. (26″)

The rapid evolution of Picasso's genius is illustrated by the fact that this portrait of the art dealer Ambroise Vollard is chronologically so close to his 'Queen Isabeau'. Less than a year has elapsed, and yet the artist has already abandoned the closed-in forms for which he had been seeking. Cézanne's lesson of the geometrization of nature is forgotten in favour, first of forms outlined by bristling crests and subsequently of these subtle bevellings, these unfinished lines, these planes no sooner indicated than forgotten as though absorbed into infinity. Picasso is now engaged in synthetic Cubism, an epoch of careful scaffolding, a patient assemblage of glass fragments. To judge by other portraits of Vollard, particularly those by Cézanne and by Renoir, by Bonnard's sketches and by existing photographs, this portrait is a good likeness. Vollard is said to have made money in his sleep, leading his clients to believe he dropped off in their presence because he was so little interested in selling. Here, then, we see the real Vollard, in process of making his fortune.

The difficulty was to introduce this assemblage into a setting which, all contemporary critics insisted, bore some relation to reality, but which, in spite of the vague outline of a bottle, we now feel to be completely abstract, created purely for pleasure. Whatever faint echo of reality may remain, the intention has clearly been towards abstraction. Out of these myriad merging facets, resembling those of a diamond faintly tinged with grey, dun or green, emerges a human physiognomy. If this face succeeds in imposing itself on the picture it is because it is similarly constructed, the whole painting echoing the broken rhythms of which it is composed, denting and curving the surface, bringing it to life in to-and-fro movement as compulsive as breathing. It is perhaps a proof of Picasso's skill that he was able to perform this exercise without the slightest trace of boredom. This is probably because this game of facets was his own invention, but his facility is none the less remarkable. Facility is, moreover, essential to Picasso, always as spontaneous as he is perfectionist.

Ambroise Vollard began to take an interest in Picasso soon after his Blue Period but in spite of this portrait he was never very convinced by Cubism.

Formerly Morosov Collection.

Ugolino da Siena
The Crucifixion

Perugino
Portrait of a young man

Domenico Mancini Portrait of a man

Francia
The Virgin and Child with two Saints

Raphael
The Virgin and Child with St Joseph

Andrea del Sarto The Virgin and
Child with SS. Catherine, Elizabeth
and John the Baptist

Vincenzo Catena The Virgin and Child with
SS. Peter and John the Baptist

273

G. B. Cariani The seduction

Lorenzo Lotto Portrait of a woman

Giorgione Judith

Titian Christ carrying the Cross

School of Titian Salvator Mundi

Licinio A widow with her three sons

Titian Saint Sebastian   *School of Titian* The Flight into Egypt

Sebastiano del Piombo
Christ carrying the Cross   *Sebastiano del Piombo* Pietà   *Paolo Veronese* Pietà

Tintoretto The Birth of St John the Baptist

Paolo Veronese The Conversion of St Paul

Annibale Carracci
The Rest on the Flight into Egypt

Annibale Carracci Self-portrait

Domenico Fetti Portrait of an actor

Guido Reni The Youth of the Virgin

Guido Reni
The Building of Noah's Ark

Domenico Fetti Tobias Healing his Father

Salvator Rosa Portrait of a man

Salvator Rosa The Prodigal Son

G. M. Crespi Self-portrait

Francesco Guardi Venice

G. B. Tiepolo
Mucius Scaevola before Porsenna

G. B. Tiepolo
The Triumph of the Emperor

Holbein Portrait of Erasmus

Lucas Cranach the Elder Portrait of Cardinal Albrecht of Brandenburg

Lucas Cranach the Elder
The Madonna of the Apple-tree

Lucas Cranach the Elder
Venus and Cupid

Lucas van Leyden
The Healing of the Blind Man of Jericho

Peter Bruegel the Elder The Fair

Anthonis Mor
Portrait of a man

Jan Bruegel the Elder Country road

Rubens Susanna and the Elders

Rubens
The Descent from the Cross

Rubens The Descent from the Cross

Rubens
The Coronation of the Virgin

Rubens Sketch for the
Adoration of the Shepherds

Rubens Sketch for the
Apotheosis of James I

Rubens
The Union of Earth and Water

Van Dyck Saint Peter

Van Dyck Portrait of a man

Van Dyck
Rubens with his son, Albert

Van Dyck
Portrait of Philadelphia and Elizabeth, daughters of Sir Thomas Cary

Frans Snyders The concert of birds

Jan Fyt Fruit and a parrot

Gerard van Honthorst The Childhood of Christ

Gerard van Honthorst Woman at her toilet

Jordaens The Royal Banquet

David Teniers the Younger Village holiday

Barthel Bruyn
Portrait of a lady
with her daughter

Dirck Jacobs Group portrait of the Civic Guards of Amsterdam

*Maerten van
Heemskerck* Calvary

Pieter Lastman Abraham journeying to the Land of Canaan

Frans Hals Portrait of a man

Hendrik Terbrugghen The concert

Jan van Goyen The River Maas near Dordrecht

Jan van Goyen Sailing-boats

Jan van Goyen Winter landscape near The Hague

Rembrandt The Parable of the Labourers in the Vineyard

Rembrandt
The Descent from the Cross

Rembrandt Portrait of a girl

Rembrandt Portrait of a young
man with lace collar

Rembrandt The Samaritan Woman

Rembrandt
Woman in front of a mirror

Rembrandt Portrait of an old woman
with spectacles in her hand

Rembrandt
Portrait of an old man in red

Rembrandt Portrait of an old man

Rembrandt
Portrait of Baartje Doomer

Rembrandt Portrait of a man

Rembrandt Girl trying on an ear-ring

Rembrandt David and Uriah

Rembrandt
Portrait of Jeremias Decker

Rembrandt Return of the Prodigal Son

Jan Asselyn Landscape with ruins

Pieter Claesz Breakfast

Adriaen van Ostade
Village musicians

Philips Wouwerman Horse-riding in the open

Jan Both Italian landscape

Adam Pynacker Boat on a river

Ferdinand Bol Game

Willem Kalf Still-life

Gabriel Metsu The Doctor's visit   *Gabriel Metsu* Breakfast

Paulus Potter The wolf-hound   *Paulus Potter* The farm

Gerard Ter Borch The messenger   *Gerard Ter Borch*
The glass of lemonade

Jan Steen The Doctor's visit

Jan Steen The drinkers

Jacob Isaackz van Ruisdael The house among the dunes

Jan van der Heyden A fortress

Aelbert Cuyp Sunset

Aelbert Cuyp The dairymaid

Francisco Ribalta
The Crucifixion

Juan Bautista Maino
The Adoration of the Shepherds

Zurbaran St Lawrence

Ribera Saint Sebastian and Saint Irene

Murillo St Anthony of Padua

Murillo The Rest on the Flight into Egypt

Velasquez
Portrait of Count Olivares

289

William Dobson Portrait of Van der Dort

Reynolds Cupid untying the Girdle of Venus

Gainsborough
Portrait of the Duchess of Beaufort

Lawrence Portrait of Metternich

Raeburn
Portrait of Mrs Eleanor Bethune

François Clouet
Portrait of the Duke of Alençon

Mathieu le Nain Peasants in a tavern

Poussin Moses striking the Rock

Poussin Nymph and Satyr

Poussin Landscape with Polyphemus

Claude Lorrain Evening *or* Tobias and the Angel

Claude Lorrain Morning *or* Jacob with Leah and Rachel

Le Sueur
The Presentation of the Virgin in the Temple

Mignard
Portrait of Hortense Mancini (?)

Rigaud Portrait of a learned man

Rigaud Portrait of Fontenelle

Antoine Watteau
The Rest on the Flight into Egypt

Lancret The kitchen

Lancret A meeting in the park

Chardin Grace before dinner

Chardin The washerwoman

Boucher Landscape with a pond

Boucher Pastoral scene

Fragonard The farmer's children

Fragonard The snatched kiss

Greuze Girl in a cap

Vigée-Lebrun Portrait of a woman

Hubert Robert The ruined terrace

Girodet Self-portrait   *Ingres* Portrait of Count Gouriev   *Horace Vernet* Self-portrait

Delacroix Lion-hunt in Morocco   *Theodore Rousseau* Market in Normandy

Corot Landscape   *Corot* Landscape with a lake

Renoir Head of a woman

Renoir Woman in black

Renoir Portrait
of Jeanne Samary

Millet Women carrying firewood

Alfred Sisley Windy day at Seneux

Vincent Van Gogh The cottages

Gauguin Fatata Te Moua. Landscape with a galloping horseman

Gauguin Eu Haere Ia Oe. Woman with fruit

Gauguin Tahitian pastoral scene

Gauguin Tahitian landscape

Gauguin Man gathering fruit

Gauguin Scene of Tahitian life

Gauguin Rave Te Hiti Aamu. Blue idol

Gauguin
Women by the sea shore

Gauguin Three women against a yellow background

Gauguin The sunflowers

Camille Pissarro The Boulevard Montmartre, Paris

Cézanne Self-portrait

Cézanne Still-life with fruit

Cézanne Pine-tree near Aix

Cézanne Flowers in a vase

Cézanne The smoker

Cézanne Still-life with a curtain

Henri Rousseau The port of Vanves

Bonnard Spring

Bonnard Landscape with a goods train

Bonnard A corner of Paris

Bonnard Landscape in the Dauphiné

Bonnard Landscape with a river

Vuillard Interior   *Marquet* Place de la Trinité, Paris

Marquet Harbour of Saint-Jean-de-Luz   *Marquet* The port of Menton

Marquet Milliners   *Marquet* Rainy day in Paris

Derain Study for the portrait
of the girl in black

Derain Man with a newspaper

Derain
Earthenware jug and white napkin

Derain Still-life with curtain

Derain The harbour

Derain Table and chairs

Derain Still-life with a skull

Matisse Still-life with a coffee-pot

Matisse Soup tureen and coffee-pot

Matisse Crockery and fruit

Matisse The Bois de Boulogne

Matisse View of Collioure

Matisse Woman on a terrace

Matisse Still-life with a pink statuette

Matisse The painter's family

Matisse Entrance to the Casbah

Matisse
Amido, the Moroccan

Matisse Moroccan man in green

Picasso Portrait of Soler

Picasso The absinthe drinker

304

LIST OF ILLUSTRATIONS

Page numbers in italic denote colom plates

313

INDEX OF NAMES

Numbers in italics refer to the notes accompangying the colour plates

318